For

Hugh Westheuser

Free Spirits

from
Bern Will Brown

Dec. 31, 2007

D1707022

Free Spirits

Portraits from the North

BERN WILL BROWN

NOVALIS

© 2007 Novalis, Saint Paul University, Ottawa, Canada

Cover image: "Moonlight Journey," by Bern Will Brown
Cover design and layout: Dominique Pelland
Interior photographs: page 20: Jackson/NWT Archives/N-1979-004:0136;
page 36: Fleming/NWT Archives/N-1990-006:0178; pages 41, 98, 123, 141:
Bern Will Brown; page 48: Sacred Heart Parish/N-1992-255:0155; page
61: Missionary Oblates, Grandin Collection at the Provincial Archives of
Alberta, OB.11464; page 72: Missionary Oblates, Grandin Collection at
the Provincial Archives of Alberta, OB.3501; pages 87, 94: Photos.com;
page 106: Fleming/NWT Archives/N-1979-050:0944; page 112: Mikilaaq
Centre; page 130: Missionary Oblates, Grandin Collection at the Provincial
Archives of Alberta, OB.30366

Business Offices:
Novalis Publishing Inc.
10 Lower Spadina Avenue, Suite 400
Toronto, Ontario, Canada
M5V 2Z2

Novalis Publishing Inc.
4475 Frontenac Street
Montréal, Québec, Canada
H2H 2S2

Phone: 1-800-387-7164
Fax: 1-800-204-4140
E-mail: books@novalis.ca
www.novalis.ca

Library and Archives Canada Cataloguing in Publication

Brown, Bern Will, 1920–
      Free spirits : portraits from the North / Bern Will Brown.

ISBN 978-2-89507-900-2

      1. Canada, Northern–Biography. 2. Adventure and adventurers–
Canada, Northern–Biography. I. Title.

FC3957.B76 2007   971.9009'9   C2007-905066-2

Printed in Canada.

We acknowledge the financial support of the Government of Canada
through the Book Publishing Industry Development Program (BPIDP)
for our publishing activities.

5   4   3   2   1   11   10   09   08   07

Contents

Foreword

Bern Will Brown:
A Passion for the North,
a Love for Its People

I first got to know Bern Will Brown through his writing and photography. I was editor of *Oblate Missions* magazine in the 1960s, his writing and photographs were an editor's delight and grist for the mill. We began a correspondence that eventually resulted in the editing and publication of his two-volume *Arctic Journal* by Novalis in 1998 and 1999. (The two books were published as one volume in 2003.)

In *Free Spirits*, Bern offers a selection of stories – by turns tragic, humorous and heart-warming – of some of the characters he has met or heard tell of during his fifty-plus years in Canada's far North. But before you get acquainted with them, take a few moments to get to know the author, a fascinating northern character himself.

Bern Will Brown, a successful painter and author, was born in Rochester, New York, in 1920. He grew up in a family of devout Catholics, and counted several priests and nuns among his uncles and aunts. His father was an avid outdoorsman who loved fishing and hunting. Living only a few feet from the water, the children learned to swim early in life. They also had a canoe, a sailboat and an outboard motor. By age twelve Bernard was running a muskrat trapline and catching the odd skunk. He took a mail order course in taxidermy.

About this time he became very interested in art, for which he was showing some talent. His parents enrolled him in a Saturday class for beginners where he began with graphite sketches, then pen and ink, watercolour, and finally oil. He liked it so much that he spent every spare minute in his room painting. Some of those early works still survive.

As soon as Bernard could handle a high-powered rifle, he joined his father on his annual fall deer hunts in the Adirondack Mountains. In the summer of 1936, when Bernard's brother Justin was fourteen and Bernard a year-and-a-half older, they spent forty-six days paddling seven hundred miles in Ontario. The following summer they used a birchbark canoe on a trip farther north in the province of Quebec. In high school Bernard read all the books in the Rochester Public Library about the far North.

In his last year of high school, Bernard took a civilian flying course conducted by the U.S. Army at the University of Rochester. Their long-range plan was to have flying instructors ready in case the United States joined World War II. Although he did get his private license that year and went on the following year to take the advanced acrobatic course, flying as a career didn't appeal to him.

During his four years of high school at Aquinas Institute, one of the Basilian Fathers who ran it suggested to him privately that he might be a candidate for the priesthood. Prompted no doubt by his mother's example and by her words, the idea had been germinating in his mind.

On a hunting trip in the Adirondacks as a young man he met a man named Nels Defendorf who regaled him with stories of a winter's hunting trip in Alaska. Defendorf spoke glowingly of gold mining and of jobs awaiting the venturesome. These stories so fired young Bernard's imagination that he talked a classmate into hitchhiking with him to Alaska after graduation from high school. They got as far as Seattle, but all northbound ships were tied up by a lengthy longshoreman's strike and they had to scrap their plans.

But the dream did not die. With his heart fixed on the North he joined the Oblates of Mary Immaculate, an order of priests and brothers renowned for their work in Canada's Far North. The very idea of spending another nine years in school seemed beyond his endurance. On the other hand, he thought he might regret it later in life if he didn't at least give the religious life a try. He said his good-byes and hitchhiked to Buffalo. Although his superiors tried to dissuade him from following his dream to work in the North, he remained firm. After being ordained as a priest in 1948, the way was clear. He was heading north.

He left Rochester at the end of that summer, driving a two-ton truck full of medical and other supplies for the northern missions. At Edmonton he continued by rail, his truck on a flatcar and himself in a Pullman. Arriving at Waterways, the end of the line, he drove the last three miles to the most southerly mission of the Mackenzie Vicariate, Fort McMurray, which is renowned today as the site of the tar sands, reputedly the largest oil deposit in the world. Eventually he landed at Fort Smith, the administrative centre of the vast Northwest Territories and the headquarters for the Catholic missions. Here he met his new boss, Bishop Joseph Trocellier, OMI. Trocellier was French born, Roman educated, and head of the Church in the North.

Bernard's enthusiasm for the North must have been infectious, for his brother Justin gave up a good business back home in Rochester and joined the Oblates as a non-ordained brother; he was making his novitiate in nearby Fort Providence. (His other brother, Thomas, would soon follow, engaging himself as a deckhand on the mission supply boat on the Mackenzie River before entering the Oblate order. Where Bernard would spend his priestly life in the frigid Canadian North, Thomas would spend his as a priest in tropical Brazil!)

Trocellier, delighted to have the two young brothers in his vicariate, sent Bernard to visit Justin in Fort Providence. They gave each other encouragement as they shared their hopes and dreams for the future. On Bernard's return to Fort Smith, the fatherly bishop assigned him to the Native mission at Fort Norman, under the tutelage of the wise and kindly Father Jean Denis. He was thrilled to accept his first formal assignment.

At Fort Norman, Father Denis met him at the plane with dog team and sled, the normal means of overland transportation in the North at the time. He immediately handed Bernard the reins and told him to drive. Careening down a steep, twisting trail into town the newcomer fell off not once but twice. He had arrived.

Young Bernard, who had believed he was finished
with book learning, now found himself studying two
languages: French, the language of the missionaries,
and Hareskin, the language of the people. For the
latter, no dictionary or grammar existed; the man
who was tired of books now had to make his own
dictionary.

After his apprenticeship, Bernard was assigned
to Fort Franklin, upriver from Fort Norman on
Great Bear Lake. There he showed his gift for car-
pentry by constructing a new mission building with
classic lines of his own design, topped by a cupola
covered in copper sheathing. It was a superb ef-
fort, strikingly beautiful. This was the first of many
new missions and churches that he would build in
the North; others were built at Camsell Portage,
Uranium City, Nahanni Butte and Colville Lake,
where he re-established a Native community that
had dispersed, building a village of log dwellings,
church, nursing station and fishing lodge. He lives
there still.

Assigned to Aklavik, the most northerly community on the Mackenzie River, he started a monthly
newspaper, *The Aklavik Journal*, which he printed on
an old Gestetner he had uncovered in an attic. He
gathered news by talking to people at Stan Peffer's
café and wherever people gathered. He published
news from the RCMP, the court dockets, advice

from the local doctor, the DEW Line, the liquor sales figures, the price of furs, the doings of town council, and notable weather information, such as the -60° Fahrenheit temperature reading on February 16, 1956. He also wrote challenging editorials and welcomed letters to the editor. Everyone had to have a copy of this exciting monthly newspaper. And that included not only the people of Aklavik and area, but the Department of Foreign Affairs in Ottawa as well as newspapers in Toronto and Vancouver. It was even quoted in Parliament. *The Aklavik Journal* was practically the only source of news from the North at a time when the North was in a ferment of transition.

The life of a Catholic missionary in the Arctic and Subarctic in the last century was one of the most difficult, lonely and challenging vocations ever in the history of Christianity. Often living in isolation for long periods of time, getting mail once a year, having to adapt from a home of comfort and ease in a temperate climate to a new language and a life and culture of harsh subsistence in a cruel and unforgiving land, Bernard persevered, adapted and became an Eskimo with the Eskimos, an Indian with the Indians. All the while he drew enormous strength from his faith, bringing Christ in his person to the ends of the earth. It is a poetic and heroic concept, but who could live it? Amazingly, many did.

But times were changing and questions were being asked. When the Catholic Church embarked on its Second Vatican Council (1962–65), hopes for change were in the air. Articles appeared in Catholic periodicals hinting that the Roman Catholic discipline of clerical celibacy might be modified to allow priests living in isolation in harsh climates to marry. Bernard Brown, in touch with these ideas, found they better reflected the reality of the North of his time. Celibacy was a concept foreign to the Eskimo and Indian, who regarded an unmarried man as less of a man. The Canadian bishops petitioned Rome to allow a married clergy for the North.

It is in this context that Bernard Brown, now in his 40s, came to the mature decision to petition Rome for permission to marry. He hoped to be allowed to continue ministering as a priest once he was married, but this was not to be.

It was not a decision he took lightly, for he cherished his role as priest and strongly identified with it. He was living in Colville Lake above the Arctic Circle when permission to marry was granted. He urged his bishop, Paul Piché, to come to Our Lady of the Snows Mission to officiate at his wedding to Margaret Steen (see story on Paul Steen p. XX), to show the natives that he was marrying with the Church's blessing. On July 19, 1971, in the log chapel that he had built, Bernard and Margaret exchanged their marriage vows before the bishop. Bern was 51.

Another priest who had taken this step might be expected to leave the North to rebuild his life in the south in his home country with his own people, as indeed a number of others from the North had done. Bernard stayed. The North was his country, the northerners his people.

But how could he survive without the support of the Church? Very well, as it turned out.

The fishing lodge he had built, and which had been in operation for a few years already, attracted wealthy fishing enthusiasts from the south during the short fishing season. He turned his talent for painting to good use, producing fine artwork depicting northern scenes. Exhibitions of his work were held in Calgary and Los Angeles, where his paintings fetched a high price and were eagerly sought, even fought over, by collectors.

Bernard Brown, at this writing, is eighty-seven years young. He still loves the North and its people. He is well respected by the priests and his bishop in Yellowknife, who regard him as a brother. He has earned the respect and admiration of the people of the North. Until recently, when he sold his plane (flying wasn't a problem, but he found it hard to climb on top of the plane to do repairs), he occasionally flew the bishop and other church officials on visits to different sites and missions (see the story of Father Frapsauce p. 59). Not long ago, he flew his brother Thomas, who has celebrated fifty years of priesthood and is still serving the Church in Brazil, on a tour of his part of the North.

In *Arctic Journal* Bern wrote, "Why is it that the North seems to be so populated with the type of person we call a 'character'?" Perhaps there are just as many in Edmonton or New York, but they are lost in the crowd. Perhaps it's the free spirit of the North that encourages people to be eccentric. Whatever the reason, I was running into an unusually large number of characters in the Territories." That statement is as good as any to launch us into the chapters that follow.

Frederick A. Miller
Ottawa

Author's Note

Over the past fifty-seven years in the North, I have encountered many interesting people who deserve to be recorded in history. Perhaps if I didn't acknowledge them they would be completely forgotten. As far as I know, none of them has left anything in writing, although their stories could have made some fascinating reading.

I got their stories by talking with them – in two cases, with the use of a tape recorder. In most cases I made notes of our conversations after I got home. I wish now that I had photographed them all, but I wasn't carrying a camera. They each impressed me so much that I recorded their stories. In the following pages you will read what I jotted down. Their stories are part of our Canadian history, and offer a glimpse of life in this remote and rugged area of our land, the far North.

Bern Will Brown
Colville Lake, 2007

Murder Most Foul:

The Axe Murders of Brother Alexis and Geneviève Duquette

The missions of the Mackenzie Vicariate in northern Canada have produced some harrowing tales of death and survival amid the ice and snow, but none as gruesome and disturbing as the murder of Lay Brother Alexis in 1875.

I spent the winter of 1951 in Fort Chipewyan waiting for the ice to break up on Lake Athabaska so I could proceed east to Camsell Portage and build Mission St. Bernard. During the winter I had been sent out to the brothers' wood camp to spend two weeks with them as chaplain. Brother Louis Crenn was their cook. Born in France in 1879, he had spent over fifty years at Fort Chipewyan, never once leaving on a vacation. We spent countless hours together, during which he told me many stories of the early days, including this one, which I carefully recorded.

* * *

Fort Chipewyan

B orn in France in 1828, Alexis Renard joined the Oblates of Mary Immaculate in 1850. Two years later he was given an obedience to the Missions of the Canadian North at Fort Chipewyan on Lake Athabaska, where he arrived in 1853. There he found Father Henri Faraud living in a small log cabin covered with spruce bark, with a small garden next to it. (Father Faraud later became a famous bishop in the North.)

For the next twenty-two years, this humble brother Alexis did all he could to help build up this mission, which became one of the largest in the North. In the process he also built a reputation for holiness that caused his next superior, Father Isidore Clut (later another famous bishop) to call him "a model of virtue." He was even invited to study for the priesthood, but in his humility he refused.

Twenty years after his arrival at Fort Chipewyan, the mission had grown so big that Sisters were needed to open a school for the Chipewyan children. Three Grey Nuns, brought down from Fort Providence, established a convent in a warehouse while they taught ten Native children in a small log cabin. Among these children was an eleven-year-old orphan named Geneviève Duquette. Three years later, in 1875, word reached Fort Chipewyan that three more nuns were on their way from their mother house in Montreal. Brother Alexis was chosen to go by skiff some three hundred miles upstream to the mission at Lac la Biche, where he was to build a scow to transport the arriving Sisters with their personal luggage and supplies down to their new posting.

Acting as guide and helper for Brother Alexis was one Louis Lafrance, a half-breed Iroquois from Caughnawaga, near Montreal. At first he was employed by the Hudson Bay Company near Fort Jasper in the Rocky Mountains. Later he moved to Lac Ste Anne near Edmonton and was hired on by the Catholic mission there. A Father Jean Tissot met him at Fort Pitt in 1861 and wrote of him in language typical of the age, "Louis the Iroquois is not a Protestant, but he is impure." In 1865 when a priest named Father Remas returned from a trip to his mission at Lac Ste Anne he found his cabin ransacked; he was told the damage had been done by Lafrance.

Soon after this episode, another Oblate took Lafrance farther north to the mission at Île-à-la-Crosse, where Cree Natives took an immediate dislike to him. They predicted, "Someday he is going to kill someone because of his violent temper." To illustrate this facet of Lafrance's personality, Bishop Vital Grandin told of the time when Lafrance got mad at his dog team because they were not travelling in a straight line. With one stroke of his axe, he chopped one unfortunate dog in half, putting one half on each side of the trail to serve as a lesson to the other teams passing.

Not only was he boastful and cruel, Lafrance was vain, too. He wore a pair of beautifully ornamented moccasins he refused to take off even at night. But on the positive side, Louis Lafrance was a good guide and hunter and, like his Iroquois countrymen, appeared attached to his religion. Bishop Clut, in one of his letters, called him "Brother Louis" and spoke of his progress in the spiritual life. Lafrance always accompanied the missionaries on their long trips in the North.

When Brother Alexis pulled away from the mission dock at Fort Chipewyan in his skiff that June day in 1875, Louis Lafrance was also at the oars, and in the boat with them was the orphan girl Geneviève Duquette, now age fourteen, on her way to the Sisters at Lac la Biche.

Melting snow in the mountains to the west had raised and quickened the opposing current. This, plus the fact that they were heavily loaded with moose hides and salt from Fort Smith, slowed their progress. It took them twelve days of steady rowing upstream to reach Fort McMurray, and another eight days to get to the Grand Rapids on the Athabaska River. They arrived on June 20. There they ran into so many floating trees uprooted by the spring flood

that they could not continue. They were also getting short of supplies.

At this point they met up with two Métis families,
the Huppes and the Trembles, who were travelling
in the same direction. These families had decided to
return downstream to Fort McMurray for supplies
and to wait for the water to drop. But Brother Alexis
knew his orders were urgent. He decided to press
on, abandon his skiff and go overland the remaining hundred miles to Lac la Biche. Although they
had only three days of supplies left, both men were
good hunters and carried their rifles. The two Métis
families noticed that the brother was having trouble
with Lafrance, who was bothering the girl. They offered to take her with them, saying that she would
be hard pressed to keep up on foot over the rough
trail. The Iroquois replied, "If she can't make it, I'll
carry her on my back." That was the last anyone ever
saw of Brother Alexis or of Geneviève Duquette.

Over a month later, on July 27, Bishop Faraud
arrived by boat at Lac la Biche and found no Brother
Alexis. The Huppe boys arrived around the same
time and reported finding the brother's blanket, coat
and gun at Grand Rapids, where they had parted.
Bishop Faraud wrote: "Twenty-six days have passed
since their last traces were found and still neither
the brother nor anyone else has appeared here." He
immediately sent out two men and four horses with

provisions to follow the bush trail the brother was thought to have taken.

One of these, Julien Cardinal, returned with this story: "When I arrived at House River I found on the bank footprints which I followed to a mound in the sand. Digging here I discovered the head of Brother Alexis. I pulled it out by the hair and noticed a bullet hole in it. Digging deeper at this mound I found burnt bones. There was no doubt in my mind that the brother had been killed and partly eaten by the Iroquois. I looked around in the bush nearby and found the remains of a campfire and in the ashes the bones of a human hand. I hurried back with this news to Father Hyppolyte Leduc at Lac la Biche."

Another four men were sent back to bring in what remained of the murdered brother. They found his bones scattered pell-mell, showing axe marks in several places, and a bloody axe nearby. Louis Lafrance had evidently cut and dried strips of flesh like one would do with buffalo meat. It was the fourth of September before Brother Lambert returned to Lac la Biche with the remains of Brother Alexis.

Bishop Faraud concluded that they had lost their way in the bush and starvation had caused the Iroquois to lose his head and resort to cannibalism. But what the bishop did not know about was the friction that had built up between the brother and his half-breed guide over the orphan girl who was travelling with them. On the following February 1 he wrote to Bishop Tache: "We are still ignorant of the whereabouts of Louis Lafrance and the orphan."

Later, some Chipewyans found a campsite in the bush where two people had slept. They also found there the moccasins of a young girl and some human bones. Evidently the Iroquois had treated Geneviève Duquette in the same way he had treated the brother.

Nine years later, Father August Husson at Peace River, Alberta, reported: "The Beaver Indians tell me about being visited by a marauder for several years. He appeared to be a white phantom who circled their tents at night. Everyone was terrified. They lost their dogs one by one. They lost meat and fish from their stages. He was a great mystery because, unlike Nakani, their legendary wild man, he travelled in winter and therefore left tracks in the snow. One night a Beaver Indian who had lost a dog to the phantom fired at the mysterious form as it climbed to his cache of meat. He dove back into his tent before he could tell if he had scored. The next day he followed a trail of blood a short way into the bush and found a dead Indian, thin and ragged, dressed in clothes made of tent canvas. Upon further inspection it was discovered that his big toes were missing, probably from frostbite. Most revealingly, around his neck he was wearing the bronze cross of an Oblate lay brother. Thinking that he had shot a brother this Indian quickly buried the body and told no one of the incident. It was nine years before these Indians heard of the death of Brother Alexis and told me this story."

Thanether's Revenge

During winter of 1951–52 that I spent in Fort Chipewyan, where I picked up that story of Brother Alexis from Brother Crenn, I had occasion to visit an elder Métis by the name of Francis Mandeville. He told me the remarkable story of a Chipewyan woman named Thanether, which means "marten falling down." His story went something like this.

* * *

The Crees had been age-old enemies of the Chipewyan nation, driving them west and north from their original hunting grounds. It was bad enough fighting with bow and arrow and spear, but when the Crees got rifles from the white traders at Fort Churchill on Hudson Bay, the contest was greatly in their favour. The "Chips," living farther west, had no chance to meet the whites and knew nothing of firearms.

Once upon a time, the story goes, the Chipewyans took the Crees by surprise, defeated them and seized their guns. Not knowing what to do with the guns, they cut them up and forged the metal into knives and spears.

In another battle, near the eastern end of Lake Athabaska, a young Cree chief and his warriors captured a complete Chipewyan village. They systematically sacked and pillaged it from end to end. Their rule of engagement was that no one must be left alive. However, the young Cree chief, on entering one of the teepees, saw an unusually beautiful Chip girl and, instead of killing her, covered her with a caribou hide.

When the slaughter was over, the young chief brought forth from concealment his prize booty and told the others he intended to take her home. After some days of travel eastwards they reached their village. The young chief approached his father timidly and confessed how he had broken their rule of engagement to take no prisoners. He presented his prize and said that he had decided to take her for his wife. His father yielded to his son's request, and the young chief and the Chipewyan woman were married according to the tribal ritual.

Thanether soon justified her husband's choice. She proved herself a better woman than the Cree wives – more clever in sewing and woodcraft – and she soon mastered the Cree language. Best of all, she bore the young chief two sons.

Although she seemed to be living a happy life
with her Cree enemies, Thanether never forgot
the murder of her people. In her heart she secretly
determined to vindicate them somehow. She noted
that these people made long trips to Churchill in
the spring to trade their furs. She felt that if she
could learn where they got their guns and could get
this news back to her Chipewyan tribe, they could
be saved from total extermination. So she conceived
her plan. She decided to risk all and follow the men
when they left on their annual trading trip.

The day after the men left, Thanether slipped
out quietly at night. She carried only a caribou robe
and some dried meat. The trail left by the men was
visible enough, and she had little difficulty overtak-
ing them on the third day out. But she had to keep
back for fear of being detected. On the fifth day
she noted the ground was slowly going downhill.
When she came to a stretch of open country she
could see a vast sea ahead: Hudson Bay!

Thanether followed the men right down to the
Hudson Bay Company stockade, but waited, hidden in the trees, until nightfall. When the coast was
clear she slipped into the rear of the compound and
waited. Soon the Hudson Bay factor found her and
got his Chipewyan interpreter to ask her what she
wanted. She poured out the whole bloody story of
the attack on her village and how the Crees with

their firearms were able to kill off the people so easily.

The effect of her story on the factor was immediate and profound. He called all the Natives into the Fort on the following day and berated the Cree for what they had been doing behind his back. The guns were for game, not for war. He forbade them ever to kill another Chipewyan and he stopped selling them guns. Finally he sent Thanether back to her people with an armed escort to invite them to trade.

The Irish Millionaires and Other Characters

The uranium mining boom around Uranium City, Saskatchewan, produced in the early 1950s its own crop of characters. I was fortunate to be right in the middle of it, closing the old mission at Goldfields and building the new missions at Camsell Portage and Uranium City. Travelling as I did by dog team during the long winter months, I got to meet everyone.

* * *

Eldorado Mining, a Crown Corporation, held federal jurisdiction over all the ground along the north shore of Lake Athabaska. The company didn't open it up to general staking until they had first checked it over carefully themselves, mostly by airborne scintillometers. When this ground was thrown open to the public for uranium staking in August 1952, one of the first to stake a claim was young Patrick Hughes from County Down, Ireland. The fact that he had been employed by Eldorado as a bricklayer and knew nothing about geology did not deter him. He got some of his Irish buddies to join him and they soon staked claims all over the country. Veteran stakers described most of these as "moose pasture," a term indicating its worthlessness. In spite of this, Hughes and his group were successful in selling so many of their claims that they soon quit their jobs at Eldorado. Within two years they were all millionaires! They took their money back to Ireland, where they continued staking claims for base metals and soon opened two mills in Dublin. For the grand opening they chartered a 707 in Edmonton and flew all their old friends over to join them in Ireland.

Pat Hughes was not the only one to get rich on the uranium boom. Albert Zeemil and Walter Blair were living in a tent at Crackingstone Point when I visited them by dog team. They were prospecting in that area for Gilbert LaBine, who had successfully staked uranium claims on the east shore of Great Bear Lake in the early thirties. It was not long before Zeemil and Blair struck it rich on Crackingstone and sent LaBine a telegram that said, "We have shot the elephant!" I ran into the two of them some months later when they were acting as stevedores, unloading a barge at Beaverlodge Lake. I asked Albert what they got from LaBine for staking what became

Gunnar Mine. The answer was 100,000 shares of the stock, which was soon trading for $20 a share.

Johnny Nesbitt was a pilot, prospector and partner of LaBine's. He was kind enough to fly Pat Hughes and some of his pals over to Camsell on weekends to help me build the log mission there. He had a new Beaver aircraft on floats that he kept on Martin Lake near Uranium City. One morning he was down there getting ready for a flight. He had parked his four-year-old son in his seat as he stood on a float and pulled the prop through. Unfortunately his son turned the ignition key on and the engine fired, breaking Johnny's arm with the spinning prop and throwing him into the lake, badly wounded.

Perhaps the most colourful character in the area at the time was Gus Hawker, who ran a general store. Gus had split from his Native wife in Fort McMurray; he took with him their five kids, four of whom he had named after months of the years: April, May, June and August. (I forget what the fifth one was called.) Gus's store operated from a tent at first, and it always looked as if a tornado had hit it. He kept the cash in cardboard boxes behind the counter. Customers had to pick their way around the open boxes of grub that littered the floor. Gus also bought fur from the local trappers and once took a dozen stretched beaver pelts to Buckingham

Johnny Nesbitt

Palace to present to the Queen, "in the name of all Canadians!" But none of his amusing antics could make it up with me for the child abuse he inflicted on his daughter June by taking her to wife for himself when she turned sixteen.

In 1962 I visited Louis Mercredi, who lived with his large family in Fort Smith. Louis was one of the last of the 'forerunners,' who used to precede dog teams carrying mail or freight into the North. Mail ceased to be carried by dog teams after the first aircraft appeared in 1929. But in these early days, no one seemed to have trained lead dogs to go on their own without a runner up ahead on snowshoes to break trail. Forerunners were paid less than drivers. The Hudson Bay Company paid them $110 a month plus moccasins and snowshoes. They travelled nine hours a day, with a stop every three hours to make fire, drink tea and smoke their pipes. Distances were often measured by how many pipes were smoked. These runners had handkerchiefs tied just below their knees and routinely covered 30 to 35 miles a day, depending on the depth of the snow. They never wore mukluks, only moccasins and finger gloves, and they changed their socks at each fire stop. Louis Mercredi was one of the last of a dying breed of men.

Gus Kraus and the $5 Payoff

Gus Kraus was probably the most knowledgeable bush man I ever met in the North. When I built the log church at Nahanni Butte in 1961, I ate supper with Gus and his Slave Indian wife, Mary. Afterwards, we spent the evening talking.

* * *

Gus was born in Chicago around the turn of the last century. He worked there as a drayman for the local bars and sold them a mixture of wood alcohol and secret spices that he made himself. In his early twenties he immigrated to Canada and started trapping around the Peace River country with his brother Joe. He trapped his way up to Great Slave Lake and finally ended up on the South Nahanni River. En route he had married Mary, a Native woman from Fort Liard, who was a superb bush woman in her own right. He leased

five acres at the Hot Springs upriver from Nahanni
Butte, where he spent the next twenty years trapping and prospecting.

The earth around the Hot Springs is perpetually
78° Fahrenheit, but the water bubbling up from the
spring itself is 98°F. Gus made a little dam around
the springs so one could bathe in it. He claimed
there was so much sulphur in the water your skin
would slowly peel off so that if you bathed in it
three days in a row you got an entirely new skin
covering your body that was as soft "as a baby's rear
end." For this reason Gus hoped to sell the property
to someone who would open a spa there. It never
happened.

Gus put up a log cabin with a root cellar under the floor. He raised a good crop of potatoes he
thought would last him all year, but when he put
them in his new cellar it proved so hot down there
they immediately began to sprout and spoil.

The sulphur fumes from the spring permeated
the air to such an extent that any metal exposed to
it rusted out in short order. His stovepipe sticking
out of the roof crumbled, and a rifle he left outside
was soon ruined. Such a lush growth of high bush
cranberries grew up around the spring that many
birds were attracted to it and ducks stayed around
all winter.

Just landed at Nahanni Butte. Dick Turner with eggs. Gus Kraus is to his left.

After twenty-odd years, tired of the isolation of the Hot Springs location, Gus moved downriver some thirty miles to the community of Nahanni Butte, where he built a large log home. But life in the new community presented its own special problems. Like most Native women who marry white men, Mary was very jealous of Gus. One time when she suspected him of having an affair with a teacher she fired a .22 bullet through the side of his neck to teach him a lesson. "I could have killed him if I wanted to," she said later, and being the good shot she was, she is most likely right.

Gus was not only a master of the crafts associated with the life of a hunter and trapper, but he also excelled at work traditionally associated with the female sex. For example, he made great bread and could tan a moose hide as well as or better than most women. In fact, he had me write down the twenty-one steps he followed to tan a moose hide.

When he got a hold of a type of glue called Speed-Sew that was used to repair torn cloth he was completely enamored of it. He claimed that if he had discovered it earlier, he wouldn't have had to get married! He wrote this endorsement to the company selling the product and asked them to send him five tubes. They replied that if he allowed them to use his letter as a testimonial they would pay him $5. Gus wrote back telling them in glowing terms how Speed-Sew had helped him out in the bush to repair a hole in his moccasins, shirt, etc. He ended up saying never mind the $5, just send more Speed-Sew. They sent him their product plus the $5.

Gus had learned well how to build a canoe using spruce bark instead of birch bark, and could also whipsaw lumber from spruce logs. He produced boards with which he built a neat skiff. He may have been the last man in the North to master and use this technique. He also mastered the art of making the traditional Indian teepee, a picturesque feature of the North that has now died out. He described to me in great detail how one goes about sewing together twenty-four moose hides, how to stitch them together so they will shed the rain, how to arrange the top flap so that the smoke is drawn out, not to mention the arrangement of spruce around the perimeter to create a draft and the type of wood to burn to avoid sparks. "You always sleep with your feet toward the fire in the centre," he concluded. Gus knew what he was talking about.

The Newhouse steel trap was made in Niagara Falls and sold by the pound. The No. 6, for grizzly bear, weighed 44 pounds, but Gus preferred to build his own from green poles. Its dimensions were critical: narrow enough so the bear couldn't turn around, low enough so he couldn't break the top with his powerful shoulders. He had no need to follow a bear dragging a steel trap attached to a log drag. In his trap it could live for days undamaged. Gus got a lot of bears using his ingenious trap.

Gus would go on, hour after hour, telling me how to make sinew for sewing from the back muscle of the caribou, how to smoke meat to preserve it, and so on, until late into the night. Finally, I would get so sleepy I would have to excuse myself and return to my cabin.

One summer the then prime minister of Canada, Pierre Trudeau, came down the Nahanni River by canoe and met Gus. He told him that the government was going to make a national park in the upper river, including an area where Gus had his cabin at the Hot Springs. He offered Gus $6,000 for his lease and promised he would move him to any new place he chose. Gus figured he had no choice so he accepted the money and decided to move to Little Doctor Lake, about forty miles toward Fort Simpson. There he built another large cabin where he lived until he and Mary retired to the old folks' home in Simpson, where Mary still lives.

The Misadventures of Albert Faille

Albert Faille was a contemporary of Gus Kraus who trapped and prospected the same area up the South Nahanni River. Albert had left a wife and child in Minnesota and was so sure he would return soon he never became a Canadian citizen. He used to send his wife all his fur money and would visit her every few years. When he found another man had moved in with her he stopped both his visits and his money.

* * *

The Indians called Albert *Klayere dekose* – Red Pants – because one year when he needed to make himself a new pair of pants all he had on hand was red stroud. Stroud (named for a place in England) was a coarse woollen cloth or blanket common in the North in those days. But Albert was more famous in the North for his unremitting pursuit of gold, which he never found in any quantity. His relentless search came to the attention of the

National Film Board, which made him the subject of a movie.

When he walked, Albert had a pronounced stoop, which most people attributed to his many hours carrying a heavy packsack. Gus had another explanation. One time when the two were trapping up the Nahanni, Albert failed to keep a rendezvous, so Gus snowshoed to his cabin to check on him. Gus was alarmed when he saw that no smoke was coming from the stovepipe, but he found Albert safe in bed. He was crippled from a bad leg. Gus sat down by a little table that was littered with what seemed to be old prunes. "Albert, why don't you get rid of these old prunes?" he asked. Albert replied that what were on the table were actually the burned tobacco he had scraped out of his pipe bowl and was saving in case he ran out of fresh tobacco. Gus figured that chewing those tobacco heels had burned up Albert's stomach so much he had a permanent stoop.

Although Albert had an unusual number of accidents in the bush, he lived to a good old age. On a trip to Fort Simpson, Albert pulled his canoe up at the first rapids on the Liard River and was having lunch on the shore when the canoe drifted away and overturned in the rapids, dumping his outfit in the water. In 1959 he swamped in the South Nahanni River and lost everything again, including $600 in cash – which was no use on his trap line anyway. He lived on berries for eight days before an oil company helicopter spotted him. On another canoe trip downriver to Fort Simpson, he stopped for lunch on an island and then forgot his grub box there. It was after freeze-up before he got back from Fort Simpson. He still had that grub box in mind when he got back to his trapping cabin. He was heading out on snowshoes, without any grub, to go the 30 miles to retrieve it, when he ran into Gus. Gus dissuaded him from such a foolhardy trip. As it turned out, the bears had rifled the grub box months before.

The most humorous story told on Albert had to do with a batch of home brew. Gus told me Albert had persuaded him to help him build a wooden floor in his cabin. Gus was to whipsaw the boards from spruce trees and Albert would plane them smooth. Albert had little grub in his cabin, but luckily there was a ridge behind the cabin where spruce hens were continually feeding. It was easy to walk up there daily with a .22 and get a pair of birds.

One thing that Albert had left over in his larder from winter was a can of malt. It was enough to mix up a batch of home brew, which he did. Two weeks later the concoction was ready and they drank it at one sitting. On a hot July afternoon that jug sure hit the spot. Afterwards Gus said he was going up to the bird patch to get supper; Albert said he would cross the river and check his bear trap.

Gus Kraus and Albert Faille

When Gus got back there was no sign of Albert, although his canoe was still on the shore. Gus went ahead and cooked supper but he worried about Albert's absence. He went down to the shore and yelled. No answer. He walked over to the planing bench. Sticking out of the huge pile of shavings were two moccasins! He pulled on them and Albert came out with them. Then he pieced the story together. Albert, having gotten drunk on the brew, luckily forgot about crossing the river and staggered back to his planing bench. He took hold of the plane, made one long pass along the plank he had been working on, went right off the end and buried himself in the pile of shavings. Not a perfect ending to the day, but at least Albert Faille survived another of his misadventures.

Tragedy at McMillan Lake

Five Prospectors Set out with High Hopes; Only Two Returned

The area around the Nahanni River has probably been prospected more than any other in the Northwest Territories – mostly for gold. Gus Kraus did his share, and knew many who preceded him. He debunked some of the stories, such as the one of Headless Valley. The corpses of the two dead prospectors found there could easily be linked to local bears, according to Gus. Although gold has been found over a wide area, no deposit has been located to date that would justify opening a mine.

* * *

During the summer of 1959, five prospectors from Yellowknife landed at Nahanni Butte and had supper with Gus Kraus. They said they were on their way to McMillan Lake, a few miles west of the Nahanni River, to spend the winter prospecting. They had five sled dogs with them. They left a note with Gus saying a Yellowknife pilot, Chuck McIvoy, would come and get them if anything happened.

A couple of months later Frank Bailey, the game warden at Fort Simpson, flew into Nahanni Butte, picked up Gus and proceeded to MacMillan Lake to check on the prospectors. Finding three new traps in a warehouse, Bailey seized them, as this party had no trapping licence. He also found a few spruce hens in the cabin; he seized them, too, and made all the prospectors take out bird licences, which he produced from his packsack. To pay the $2 fee they borrowed from Alex Meiskonen, one of the five, who lent the money reluctantly, grumbling that he might never get it back. When Bailey found a couple of carcasses of woodland caribou on the outside stage, he made the prospectors sign a statement saying they did not absolutely need this meat. Then he loaded all the meat he could carry into his Cessna 180 and took off.

About a week later, Bailey flew back with Gus and found a fresh kill of caribou on a nearby lake.

He accused the men of breaking the game law and told them they would have to face charges when they got back to Fort Simpson. They protested that there was a new law permitting prospectors to kill game animals without a special licence. That ruse didn't last long. Bailey checked it out with headquarters in Yellowknife. There was no such law.

During the long winter months, the prospectors kept themselves busy digging an adit, or tunnel, into the bank of the creek close to their cabin, but found nothing. They were also running low on grub. Meiskonen set snares for rabbits, but caught few. When they ran out of dog food they killed their dogs and threw their carcasses in the creek. Later on, they were forced by hunger to dig out the dogs and eat them.

The situation kept deteriorating into April, when the group made the decision to send the two strongest out for help. They took what remained of their grub and left to walk overland to Fort Simpson. Their bodies were never found. Meiskonen kept visiting his rabbit snares daily. One day he got only one hundred feet from the cabin when his packsack blew up, killing him instantly. Later, when Gus examined the spot, he noted that the man's eyeglasses as well as his rifle and binoculars had been blown into a nearby spruce tree. He deduced that a stick of dynamite with a long fuse had been put in Meiskonen's

backpack by his two partners. They must have lit it
just as he was leaving the cabin. Apparently they
held a grudge against him. Was it for the petty $2
bird licenses? Perhaps he had bankrolled the whole
miserable expedition and they resented his power
over them? Whatever went wrong between them
we will never know. But Meiskonen was dead and
the two were never charged.

In May, Chuck McIvoy was flying in the area
and landed on the frozen lake to see how the prospectors were doing. He found the two survivors
barely alive and flew them out.

Later I was on a flight to Edmonton with Max
Ward. He told me that one of the two survivors,
Dean Rossworn, was suing Ward's company, Wardair,
for $10,000 for failing to fly into McMillan Lake as
they alleged they had been promised by a Wardair
pilot in a Yellowknife bar before they left on their
ill-fated expedition. Max declared that even though
no such arrangement had been made, he was forced
to pay to avoid the bad publicity just as he was to
begin international overseas flights. Gus said they
settled for $6,000.

Yukon Joe Prokop

The Quick-tempered Artist

Yukon Joe Prokop was born in Arran, Saskatchewan, about 1904, son of a trapper and prospector just like Gus Kraus, who told me this tale. But Yukon Joe did not follow in his father's footsteps. He became an itinerant artist, working his way down into the Nahanni country, painting as he went. When I was building the log church at Nahanni Butte in 1961, I noticed a couple of paintings on Gus Kraus's walls. They seemed to have been painted on cardboard. I asked Gus about them, and he told me this story.

* * *

Yukon Joe would use any kind of paint available, make brushes out of rope and work on cardboard, pieces of plywood, moose antler or whatever was handy. His inspiration didn't depend on his surroundings, but came from his head.

He had one scene he loved and repeated often: two mountains reflecting in a lake with a very red sky. His prices were dirt cheap and he would often accept room and board as part payment. Soon nearly every cabin in the country boasted a masterpiece by Yukon Joe.

One day he was riding on Cooper's barge heading up the Liard River toward Fort Nelson. He had made himself comfortable on the foredeck and was cutting down some packing cases for material to paint on. He had already completed three paintings, which were drying in the sun. Captain Cooper himself left the wheelhouse and came down to warn Joe not to get shavings in the bilge, where they could block the pump.

Joe immediately took offense and gave vent to his volatile temper. Jumping to his feet he kicked his finished paintings into the river, followed them with his paint and brushes and yelled at Cooper, "See that spruce over there? That's where I'm getting off this lousy barge!" This he did, and for pure orneriness began to hike up the bank toward Nelson. He had gotten near the village of Nietla when he saw Father Pierre Mary coming downstream in his canoe; Joe bummed a ride with him back to Nahanni Butte.

Arriving broke at Fort Nelson, Yukon Joe agreed to paint a huge mural on the wall of the local beer hall for a flat fee of $200. When he finished his painting on the second day, the proprietor argued about the price in view of the short time it had taken Joe to complete it. Joe dipped a large brush in bright red paint and yelled back, "Either you pay the $200 right now or I'll erase it!" The owner paid.

Later Yukon Joe discovered a new role. He let his hair and beard grow long, picked up a stray sled dog and could be seen shuffling along a short stretch of the Alaska Highway. He carried a packsack of new paintings on his back, and had the husky loaded with a pack of crumpled newspapers. All was calculated to make him look like a trapper who had just emerged from the bush and was on his way to the trading post. Tourists driving by would stop to take his picture, for which he charged 25 cents, and then would be shown some paintings he had for sale.

Death by Mischance

The Lonely Death
of Father Joseph Frapsauce

Death lurked for unsuspecting missionaries of the Canada's great North in the early days of missionary labour. In 1913, French Fathers Jean-Baptiste Rouvière, 32, and Guillaume LeRoux, 28, were mysteriously murdered at Coppermine, on the shore of the Arctic Ocean. Five years after their deaths, Bishop Antoine Coudert sent Father Joseph Frapsauce, age 43, to Great Bear Lake.

The area around Dease Arm of Great Bear Lake is rich in the early history of the North. About 1837, Thomas Simpson of the Hudson Bay Company built a fort at a spot about fifteen miles west of the mouth of the Dease River. Other explorers used it and it became known as Fort Confidence. Traders such as D'Arcy Arden, Joe Hodgson and Bill Boland operated trading posts near the mouth of the Dease River. Jack Hornby had a cabin a few miles west. George Douglas came in by boat in 1911 with a party of four prospectors and built a cabin three miles up the Dease River. The two Oblates Rouvière and LeRoux used it as a base before taking off on their ill-fated trip down the Coppermine River. For a while, this area had the only trading post on Great Bear Lake, and there was traffic through it by people living on the Arctic Coast en route to the nearest post office at Fort Norman. It made sense that the Church would want to station a missionary here.

* * *

Father Frapsauce built a log mission behind Rich Island some eight miles from the mouth of Dease River, where a Mr. D'Arcy Arden ran a trading post. The priest found life very lonely on Great Bear Lake, and got word to his bishop asking him to send a lay brother as a helper and companion. In 1920, the bishop chose Brother Meyer to fill the post. To accompany him north, the bishop appointed Father Pierre Fallaize. The two Oblates, priest and brother, left Fort Resolution together on the Hudson Bay sternwheeler *The Distributor*, and disembarked at Fort Norman.

At that time D'Arcy Arden happened to be at Fort Norman, where he had just taken possession of a ten-ton schooner that he intended to take up the Great Bear River to his trading post on Dease Arm of Great Bear Lake. Hearing that Father Fallaize and Brother Meyer were heading in the same direction, he invited them to accompany him on his new schooner.

Father Joseph Frapsauce, OMI

They left Fort Norman on August 12, 1920. On board were a former Hudson Bay Company trader, Bill Boland, his wife, children and dogs, several local Hareskin Indians with their families and dogs, and the two Oblates, for a total of fourteen people. The boat was crowded and heavy. They had gotten no more than three miles up the fast-flowing Bear River when they ran aground.

The dog teams and sleds were put ashore with their drivers to carry some of the freight by land. The rest of the passengers pushed the schooner against the current with long poles. It took them three weeks to get to the St. Charles rapids, halfway up the river. These rapids, which are nine miles long, run over flat limestone steps and are only about nine inches deep. The schooner, even empty, could not float through these rapids, so green spruce were cut to be placed under the keel. The boat was then slowly winched ahead with ropes and pulleys. The group spent thirteen days toiling through these rapids.

They were now into September, with the temperature below freezing and snow falling. When the party finally reached Great Bear Lake it was October 12; the ground was covered with eighteen inches of snow. Father Fallaize regretted that he had not used the mission canoe for the trip, as he could have reached his destination a month earlier by canoe.

The distance remaining was still over two hundred miles, and it was all over open water on a huge lake. D'Arcy Arden decided to leave half the weight off at Fort Franklin, four miles from the mouth of the river. The priest and brother were among those let off. Ten days later, Arden came back and picked them up. They arrived at Arden's trading post near the mouth of the Dease River on Sunday, October 24, 1920.

As the mission was situated some eight miles along the shore, Father Fallaize asked Bill Boland if he and Brother Meyer could borrow his team of dogs to go up there. Boland refused, saying his dogs didn't work on Sunday! So on Monday they got under way. Finally, the brother he had waited so long for was being delivered to Father Frapsauce.

When they finally reached the mission, they found it empty. Following fresh tracks in the snow across the lake to Rich Island, where Father Frapsauce had set up a tent to be close to his nets, they found his breviary, which had been marked for October 24. Although he was not there, he had evidently left the tent only the day before. Continuing on this puzzling path, Father Fallaize and Brother Meyer persevered. They followed more fresh tracks, which led them to the side of the lake where they saw recently broken ice a short distance from the shore. To their horror, they could make out the forms of the missing priest and his dogs floating just beneath the ice. The ice, however, was too thin and dangerous to approach. The prudent thing to do was to wait until the ice thickened. In the meantime, they drove Bill Boland's team back and announced the awful news.

The conclusion was unavoidable. If Boland had loaned his team to Father Fallaize on the Sunday, he might have reached Father Frapsauce before he took off on his fateful last trip to his nets.

To compound the tragedy, an east wind came up the next day. It was so strong, it cleared all the ice out of the bay, and with it the body of the drowned missionary and his dogs. Sobered by these events, Father Fallaize and Brother Meyer moved into the mission cabin and remained there for the next four years.

The following spring, when the snow was melting, a Bear Lake Indian by the name of Tutcho Suze was walking along the shore not far from where the drowning happened when he found some human bones and dog harness sticking out of the melting ice. Wolves or wolverines had been chewing at the carcasses and little was left. Father Fallaize and Brother Meyer carefully and reverently gathered up the remains and buried them under a large wooden cross just north of the trading post.

Bern Will Brown stands in front of the D.C.-3 that took him to Norman Wells, the northern terminus for Canadian Pacific Airlines. It was December 1948, and the temperature was 44 degrees below zero (F). He continued on to Fort Norman the next day with pilot Mike Zubko in his Waco biplane.

Bern splitting a birch root at Fort Norman, 1949. To make the handles of a toboggan people use the natural bend of a birch root for strength.

Philip Stenne and Bern working to get Mission St. Bernard closed in before freeze-up, Summer 1952.

Re-canvassing the freighter canoe (a V-stern 22-foot Peterborough).

"Arctic Reflections", Bern Will Brown

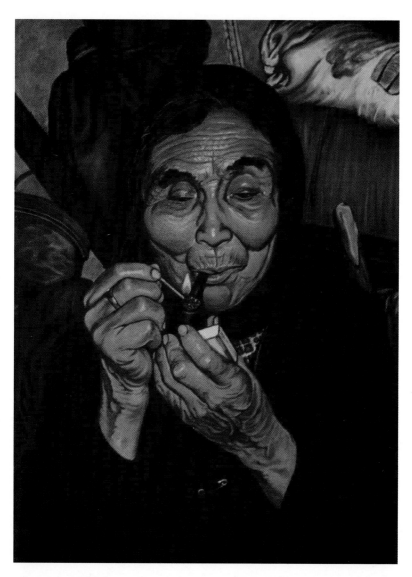

"Ahson", Bern Will Brown. The word means *grandmother* in Hareskin. The subject's name was Verona Pascal. One of Bern's tasks as the local medic was to remove and clean her glass eye weekly. She died at Colville in 1980.

"Evening chores", Bern Will Brown

"Breaking trail", Bern Will Brown. Oil on canvas. 16" x 20"

On several occasions, flying over the area in my float plane, I had tried, without success, to find that grave. Finally I received a small map from the Oblates in Paris, France, giving the exact location. With the help of that map I went there again in 1991 and found the gravesite. Two years later I flew the Oblate Provincial, Father Jacques Johnson, to the site at Dease Bay on Great Bear Lake where a lonely Father Joseph Frapsauce had died by mischance, with the help he had requested only a day's journey away. We erected at the site in the wilderness a ninety-lb granite memorial stone that we had brought with us, and left his bones to rest in the silence that had been his only companion except for his breviary, his mass and his faith.

Hamar Nelson

Lonely Traveller Memorialized by a Mountain

Hamar Nelson was a Norwegian trapper who trapped out of Baker Lake in the Eastern Arctic into the Thelon River country. Later he travelled alone via Coppermine down to Yellowknife, a very long trip. The Eskimos called Hamar "The lonely traveller." I met him in Norman Wells in 1949.

* * *

Hamar fed his dogs a supply of rabbit skins dipped in fat. He told me that his team not only survived on that diet, but actually got fat. Hamar had some odd ideas about maintaining his own health. He would go vegetarian for months and then switch to an all-meat diet. On the other hand, maybe he was not that odd after all, since a lot of people do the same switch in diet in the general population on a regular basis.

In Yellowknife, in 1919, hearing of the oil strike around Norman Wells, Hamar packed his small boat and went down there hoping to strike it rich in oil. Although he did participate in staking oil claims for the Imperial Oil Company, he never took any for himself. Instead he started prospecting for gold west of Norman Wells, over in the Mackenzie Mountains. During his summers he would do occasional work for Imperial Oil to earn a grubstake.

When Hamar told me he often built an igloo on his travels in the Barren Lands, I persuaded him to teach me the technique, for I was new in the country. For many afternoons we worked together on the banks of the Mackenzie River, where the snow is blown to the right consistency, until I learned the art.

He built several cabins in his prospecting country west of Norman Wells, but his main cabin was at Florence Lake. He was very secretive about his prospecting area and wouldn't take any men in the plane that flew him out there. He would, however, let female passengers accompany him, because in his view, "Women don't know where they are in the bush."

Hamar never found enough gold to make a mine, and died suddenly of an apparent heart attack in his cabin at Florence Lake. When he fell he tipped over a candle that partially burned him, but he was already dead. The people of Norman Wells have named a mountain after him.

Father Alexis Robin

A Man of Many Stories

Father Alexis Robin, OMI, who was born in France in 1886 and came to Fort Good Hope in 1912, was one of the Oblate missionaries who got involved in much more than preaching the gospel. He was inquisitive and inventive. During over forty years stationed at Fort Good Hope he became a beacon to his Native parishioners – not only in religion but also in living off the land. Unlike most of his contemporaries he decided late in life to write his memoirs. By this time he had been moved to Fort Resolution. Unfortunately, this work was terminated during a temporary absence when a fellow Oblate, during a cleanup of the mission, burned his manuscript. Father Robin later told me that this incident discouraged him from ever writing again. Another great historic book shot down in flames.

When I visited him in 1955 he had already been in the North for forty-three years and had years to go yet.

* * *

Father Alexis Robin, OMI

Besides his regular duties as pastor of this mission among the Hareskin Indians, Father Robin ran a trapline that took him six miles out into the bush. He also planted an extensive garden, mostly of potatoes, which he sold to the residential school hostel in Aklavik. Income from the potatoes netted him about $2200 a year, which was plenty for him and his Oblate brother assistant to live on. He also had nets set in the Mackenzie River, but was being bothered by wolves, which had learned to pull the nets out of the water and consume the fish. He tried to raise fox and marten in pens near the mission, but there was so much noise that these sensitive animals ate their own young.

He told me of a Chinese man who came in with his dog team one winter and stayed a year making lime from rocks found near the ramparts. This product was used locally to whitewash the log cabins. When this gentleman was invited to dine with the local North West Company manager, he showed up dressed in white tie and tails! Just how he carried those clothes in a dog sled was a matter of some amazement.

Father Robin told tales of voyageurs who were hired by the Hudson Bay Company to track their York boats upriver to either Grand Rapids on the Athabaska River above Fort McMurray, or to Portage La Loche on the upper Clearwater River

above the Methy Portage. These trackers became
obsolete when, in 1890, the sternwheeler *Wrigley*
began running down the Mackenzie River.

Speaking of fur, he told me of one trapper out
of Fort Rae who sold a silver fox to Bishop Breynat
and received in return a team of horses, a wagon
and harness plus flour and tea. The pelt had been
worth $1800!

Fort Good Hope was poorly situated for fish
and game. Although it had been established only
as a seasonal trading post, people ended up living
there year round. As a result, there were many lean
months in town. This situation reached crisis pro-
portions in 1841, when starvation became rampant.
The manager of the Hudson Bay Company store
was forced to take his family and retreat to Fort
Norman to find enough food to survive. When he
returned to Fort Good Hope in the spring, he discovered that fifty-two of the Indians had perished
from famine within two hundred yards of the fort.
More alarming was the fact that the survivors were
living on the carcasses of the dead! He also mentioned that the living kept an axe handy in case they
were attacked in their sleep in order to be devoured
by their relatives.

This situation made it dangerous for strangers to
visit the area. Two mail carriers from Fort Simpson,
John Spence and Murdoch Morrison, had left that

settlement in February by dog team carrying mail for Peel River Post, now called Fort McPherson. On March 18 they dropped off some mail at Fort Good Hope and continued north, following the river. Nothing more was heard from them. They completely disappeared. Only in July did the Hudson Bay Company manager write to his superior in Fort Simpson saying that he had learned that the two express men had been murdered by four women three days below Fort Good Hope. It was presumed that the two mailmen had been invited up to the women's camp to have a cup of tea. They were both hit on the head as they warmed themselves by the fire, and were subsequently made into dry meat. Only a few bones remained at the campsite.

The question of punishing these cannibals was referred to Sir John Simpson, the Governor-in-Chief of Ruperts Land in 1843. He replied that no punishment was in order because the poor women in question had been induced to commit their foul act by the most pressing calls of hunger.

Such stories as these made talking with Father Robin very interesting.

The Death of Savaar

A Sickness that Can Kill

Many of the white trappers who came into the North lived alone in log cabins scattered all over the country. Many lived around the shores of Great Bear Lake and down the Anderson River. Such a one was a Frenchman known simply as Savaar. In 1959, when he came downriver from Hay River with his canoe and dogs and went up the Bear River into Great Bear Lake, he was already sixty years of age.

* * *

Eldorado Mine maintained a sawmill on the tip of Grizzly Bear Point one hundred miles southwest of the mine, to cut lagging for the mine. Savaar chose that area to build himself a windowless log cabin. In January 1960, an RCMP dogsled patrol out of Fort Norman went to check on him, as it was a very isolated spot. To their amazement, Savaar took his rifle in hand and drove them off, saying he didn't want any visitors! The Mounties, not wanting any confrontation, left him alone, thinking he had succumbed to 'cabin fever,' a form of mental illness that was not uncommon among solitary trappers.

In May of that year, Father Félicien Labat landed at Savaar's cabin in a ski plane. There was no sign of life. Nine sled dogs were dead, tied to their posts. Inside the cabin, all that was left of Savaar were the bones of his tibia and cranium and one sled dog, which had survived by feeding on his corpse. His bones were taken to Fort Franklin for burial.

It's a mistake for a person to come to the North to fulfill some fanciful dream of solitary bliss in the pristine wilderness. Unless a person is well grounded and secure in his person, going north in search of peace is a dangerous illusion. Wherever we go, we cannot escape our inner demons. We bring them with us.

Alfred Sidene

A Hareskin Indian Discovers
a New World

Alfred Sidene, a Hareskin Indian born in 1877, was the oldest character I met in the North. When I spoke with him he lamented that everything of the days of his youth had disappeared.

By the time I met Alfred Sidene in 1962, he was old and blind. He often had one of his grandchildren lead him about the village with his cane. He would go into the Mission chapel to speak to the Lord. In a very loud voice he would recount to the Lord everything that was going on locally. Visitors who happened to be present were struck speechless by this candid recital of the day's news.

On one of his periodic visits, Dr. Dowler, the travelling dentist, arrived by ski plane. He wore his huge buffalo-skin coat, which he refused to take off because it held all the tools of his trade, including loaded hypodermic needles, in multiple pockets in the lining. When he peered into Sidene's mouth with the aid of a flashlight, he called to me, "This old bird has no teeth at all!" I replied that I knew that, but Sidene had heard that the white men could make artificial teeth and he wanted a set.

Dowler had the right material in his coat to make the impression, and that evening he cast a plaster of Paris form in my workshop. Later he sent Sidene an upper plate, but Sidene didn't like it because it cut his lower gums. Dowler wrote to me that these plates were expensive, and he wanted Sidene to get used to the upper set before Dowler sent the lower. Sidene kept these teeth in his shirt pocket, and the only time I saw him use them was just before someone took his photograph. When we buried him he still had his new uppers in his shirt pocket.

* * *

Alfred told me of a trip he and a large group of his fellow Hareskins had made to the Arctic Coast about the year 1899. They had heard from some Eskimos that a large whaling ship was frozen in at Langton Bay, three days' travel east of the mouth of the Anderson River. Moreover, the white men aboard were trading some valuable items for furs. So a large party of Hareskin Indians went down there by dog team and found the ship.

They were welcomed aboard and shown some marvellous new things never seen before, such as live pigs, and water taken from a barrel with a spigot. One of the Hareskins spoke the Eskimo language, making communication easy. Sidene said they traded fox, beaver and marten pelts for such items as Assomption sashes and canvas. It was the first time they had seen these things. The Hareskins were accustomed to covering their teepees in winter with caribou hides and in summer with moss. This was the introduction of canvas to their world! This may seem small to us today, but to them it was the beginning of many changes to come.

A group of Eskimos was camped nearby; they staged one of their typical drum dances aboard the whaler the first night. The next night the Hareskins displayed their own form of drum dancing. During the day the natives watched the whalers play a game of baseball on the ice. By the time this historic visit had ended, the weather had gotten so warm that the Indians returned to their own territory in the south, their dogs loaded down with their new acquisitions.

Tom Throne

The Softening of a Wily Rascal

Tom Throne was in his eighties when I met him at his cabin in the Mackenzie River Delta in 1956. He was raised in Texas, where he had worked as a cowboy. He fit the cowboy image, even to the six-shooter he carried.

* * *

Tom worked his way north and ended up a trapper in the delta. He had never married, but in his fifties he took a shine to fourteen-year-old Philamene, daughter of George Adams, his neighbour fifteen miles to the north.

He started visiting the Adamses on a regular basis, and on those visits paid special attention to Philamene. She was terrified when she heard Tom's kicker coming and hid herself. That bearded old white man with the strange drawl scared her out of her wits!

Tom made no bones about his intentions toward the girl. He worked tirelessly on her father to try to persuade him to consent to his daughter marrying Tom. He drew a glowing picture of the benefits to the whole family. Among other things, he mentioned a lot of money he still had in Texas, which could be of great benefit to George in his declining years. Furthermore, he said he intended to take Philamene, following the wedding, on a grand shopping spree out in Edmonton and show her sights she had never imagined. To the girl herself Tom promised blue-eyed children, the dream of every native maiden.

This persistent selling job went on summer and winter for two years. Finally, when Philamene turned sixteen, her father gave his consent. Apparently the girl had no say in the matter. Tom took Philamene over to Aklavik with his canoe and kicker for the ceremony. The Adamses were all Catholic, but Tom, never having been baptized, was, strictly speaking, a pagan! The only way the Adams family would allow the union would be for Tom to become a Catholic and be married in church. They insisted on it. He lost no time informing the priest at the Aklavik mission that he wanted to join.

Instructions began immediately and Tom threw himself into the work involved. No one around the mission could remember seeing anyone with the regularity and fervour displayed by Tom Throne as he prepared himself for baptism during the following two weeks. He attended every religious ceremony in church and could often be seen sitting out by the bank of the Peel Channel studying his catechism.

The great day finally arrived and Tom received the sacraments of baptism and marriage the same day. After the wedding, the sisters of the convent put on a grand banquet, which was followed in the evening by a dance at Peffer's Hotel. Everyone wished the newlyweds a long, happy life together. The next day Tom helped Philamene into his canoe and they headed back to his cabin on the east side of the delta to spend their honeymoon.

That honeymoon was short-lived and Philamene's dark premonitions were soon realized. She herself had fallen into one of the wily old trapper's traps. Not only did she not get to see the bright lights of Edmonton, she couldn't go anywhere, even to visit her mother, fifteen miles away. Tom soon enforced a strict obedience with a stout stick, which Philamene began to feel too often across her young back. Visitors were unwelcome at the Throne cabin. Even the Mounties were locked out. The couple had no children and Tom never entered a church again.

This was the situation twenty-one years later when I was building the first church at 'E-3,' which became the town of Inuvik. When I heard this story I was anxious to see for myself and change the situation for the better if I could. In my speedboat I went upriver to the camp of Pascal, who lived nearby the Thrones. He had never visited his neighbour because he anticipated that he would not be welcome. I persuaded him to accompany me to their camp and we went together one evening.

When we pulled up to Tom's dock we found a typical low, sod-roofed cabin on the bank of a narrow channel. There was a log warehouse nearby, plus a stage, hanging with freshly split whitefish, and numerous sled dogs chained in the yard.

Tom didn't lock his door against us, as we had feared, but came down to the dock and shook our hands. In fact, he was friendly and entertaining. It was difficult to believe that this was the same antagonistic character we had been hearing about. In spite of his age, he was not at all feeble, and told us about driving seven powerful huskies into Arctic Red River every month to get his social security cheque. Philamene came to the door to shake our hands and then busied herself poking the wood fire and making us tea.

Mackenzie River

We sat down at the table beside a window facing the river while Tom regaled us with stories of his early boyhood in Texas and his travels that had ended up here in the Mackenzie Delta. Although he knew I was a representative of the church, he never once mentioned religion. In speaking of his wife, whom he referred to as "the little girl," he said casually, "Of course I told her we'd never have any children."

If Tom lacked a friendly rapport with his fellow humans, he didn't show it with us and was certainly on friendly terms with the surrounding wildlife. To demonstrate this, as we sat at table he called a red squirrel by name. The squirrel immediately entered a small hole in the screen and ate out of his hand, followed by a whiskey jack. Later, outside, we watched fascinated as he fed some seagulls that swooped down to take bits of bannock from his hands.

Across the delta in Aklavik, where the church ran a hostel for children, there were at least a dozen orphans whom the hostel had to keep for the summer vacation time as they had no family to return to. I was always on the lookout for families who would take them. Host families would be paid a daily stipend of fifty cents.

It now occurred to me that Tom and Philamene might welcome such a child, and I promptly broached the idea with Tom. I told him I could get him an

Eskimo or an Indian boy or girl from age seven to fifteen. As we talked, Tom gradually warmed to the idea, finally agreeing to it. I followed this proposal with another that would give Philamene her first vacation away from Tom in twenty-one years. I suggested that his wife accompany me back to E-3 to receive and bring their charge home.

To this idea Tom immediately objected, saying she was needed to feed their thirteen sled dogs. I countered by arguing that such a chore should be easy for an oldtimer like himself who must have taken care of his dogs for years before he was married. Finally he said, "Well, it's up to the little girl herself." When I turned to Philamene for an answer she was already digging in a trunk and taking out a dress and bonnet. In two shakes she was dressed and down to the dock ahead of us. She was anxious to leave before Tom changed his mind. We shoved off in a hurry, leaving Tom standing on his dock looking for all the world like a lost soul.

That calm night, under the midnight sun, I first dropped Pascal off at his cabin and then went on to the Adams cabin, where we found no one at home. We headed north, which is downriver, to the new Aklavik. During the trip, Philamene gave me the whole story of her life with Tom Thorne. The more I heard, the more I congratulated myself for organizing this break for her. When we arrived and located her mother in a tent by the river, the two couldn't seem to let go of each other. What a reunion I witnessed!

The following day I got word over to the hostel at Aklavik by wireless, and was promised that they would send someone by the first available means. It took a week before a twelve-year-old boy named Paul Ipillum arrived at E-3. Two weeks had elapsed before Philamene and I could return to her cabin with the young Eskimo. We had been gone much longer than I had estimated to Tom and I feared he might be in a bad mood.

It was midnight when the three of us pulled in to Tom's dock, but he was nowhere in sight. We didn't know what to think. Was he mad? Had he left? When we got up to the closed door of the cabin, Philamene suddenly ran around to the back of the cabin. I thought she had gone to get a hidden key; when she didn't return, I followed her and found her putting moss between the logs. Apparently the door was not locked, but she lacked the courage to go in and face her husband. Finally I got her to follow me and the young boy, Paul.

We found Tom hunched over his radio, his ear close to the speaker as the battery was weak. He hadn't heard us arrive. Before he had a chance to complain of our delay I pushed Paul forward to shake his hand. Tom's eyes lit up! The crisis was over and Philamene, relieved, began building a fire in the wood stove. We ate a late supper of fried potatoes and boiled rhubarb and I left the threesome to return to my post, happy with the outcome of this little adventure.

When I returned in late August to take Paul back to school in Aklavik, I found him dressed in new clothes sewn for him by Philamene. Tom had taken him on a successful moose hunt, taught him how to set a gill net and in general had taken to him like a real son. Tom told me, "I think we'll try to adopt him legally. I can't live forever and he could have my trap line and all this equipment." It sounded like a good idea to me.

The Reindeer Station

Mikkel Polk, Reindeer Herder

Mikkel Polk was a Norwegian Saami who came to Canada to act as chief herder of the Canadian reindeer herd. His people back home in Norway had raised these animals for centuries, which gave him a natural affinity for the work.

* * *

I n the 1920s, the migrating Barren Land caribou had all but ceased coming into the Mackenzie Delta area, which meant that a vital source of wild meat was lost to the local natives. To counter this loss, the Canadian government signed a contract with the Lomen Reindeer Company of Alaska to deliver 3,442 domestic reindeer to the Mackenzie Delta. They left Alaska in December 1929, expecting the trek to take one-and-a-half to two years. It actually took five.

Reindeer

In 1933 the government set aside 17,094 square kilometres of land on the east side of the delta as the Reindeer Grazing Reserve and put up buildings and a corral thirty miles north of present-day Inuvik, in a place they called Reindeer Station.

A minimum of sixteen herders was needed to keep the animals together. Local Eskimos were hired for the work. They brought their wives and children to the Reindeer Station, which soon became a small town with its own store and school.

According to Mikkel, the life of a herder was not easy. They were obliged to work the herd on foot in summer and on skis in winter and were not allowed to carry tents out on the Barren Lands. They had border collie dogs to help with the herding. Herders were paid $20 a month to start, which increased through the years to $90 a month.

Some of the herders bought their own herds from the government and went off on their own, but by 1956 all the herds were back in government hands.

At that time the American government was building the Distant Early Warning (DEW) Line across the Canadian Arctic, paying $2.10 an hour, which was a powerful inducement for the local Eskimos. Many of the Eskimo herders left to join the DEW Line, but not Mikkel Polk.

What remains of the original reindeer herd is now in the hands of Lloyd Binder, one of Mikkel's grandsons. Both Mikkel and his wife, Anna, died in the Inuvik hospital at an advanced age. Their son, Nels, and daughter, Ellen, still live in Inuvik.

"Arctic Whaler", Bern Will Brown. Oil on canvas. 24" x 30"

"Our Lady of the Snows", Bern Will Brown. Oil on canvas. 7 x 8 feet

"Woman with Sewing Machine", Bern Will Brown. Oil on masonite. 22" x 26"
This native woman at Fort Franklin is making a set of "uppers" for a pair of slippers.

"Midnight Mass", Bern Will Brown

"The Lost Patrol", Bern Will Brown. Oil on canvas. 20" x 24"

"Under the Parhelion", Bern Will Brown. Oil on canvas. 24" x 30"

"Margaret at Her Net", Bern Will Brown

Bern Will Brown seated in front of one of his paintings.

Slim Semmler

Outstanding Trapper Outlived Them All

Lawrence Frederick "Slim" Semmler was born in Oregon at the beginning of the twentieth century and came into the North trapping north of Fort McMurray around Embarras Portage. In 1927 he joined trapper Nels Vhatum, who took him down the MacKenzie River and east along the Arctic Coast, finally dropping him off at Young's Point between Paulatuk and Coppermine.

Long before I actually met Slim, I heard stories of his superhuman strength and endurance.

Perhaps the first was the story of how he had saved the Mission schooner at Coppermine. It seems that the mission boat was stranded on a reef near the harbour. The crew had laboured in vain to free it when Slim happened by and plunged into the water. By brute strength he single-handedly lifted the bow enough for the boat to float free. Everyone was astonished.

Slim Semmler

Other stories told of his dog-driving abilities, where the dogs wore out before he did and he switched teams and kept going. I visited his isolated trading post on Cape Krusistern and wondered how he and his wife, Agnes, had braved the harsh winters there. Later, in Inuvik, Agnes became a founder of COPE – the Committee for Original Peoples Entitlement – and brokered the first treaty between the Eskimos and the federal government.

Slim ended up operating a trading post there and I used to bring him a load of whitefish from Colville Lake. True to his canny trading instincts, Slim wanted me to take my pay in trade goods from his store.

* * *

With a canvas tent as a base of operations, Slim trapped white fox with his dog team and sold his furs to the Hudson Bay Company at Bernard Harbour. The following year, 1928, he moved east to Stapleton Bay and continued trapping. Then he met Agnes, daughter of trapper Pete Norberg, and married her in Coppermine. (Pete was later lost on a spring hunt up the Coppermine River with his son Johnny, and his body was never found.)

Next, Slim bought an old trading post on Cape Krusistern, which he operated for several years with the help of his new wife. At the same time he continued trapping and was so driven in his pursuit of fur that he kept two dog teams. When he got back with one played-out team, he harnessed a fresh team and took off again.

In 1947 he moved west to the Mackenzie Delta, where he established a mink farm on the Napoyak Channel. But he ran into trouble with the game authorities when they prohibited him from feeding beluga whale meat to his mink. On top of that, a friendly bush pilot buzzed his ranch so low that his female mink got frightened and ate her young.

So Slim moved to the Hudson Bay Channel opposite Aklavik and opened another trading post. He had lost two schooners loaded with trade goods while trading on the Arctic Coast, and now sought a safer location. When the government moved Aklavik to the east side of the delta in 1955, he moved his operation there and traded out of a tent until he got a proper building up.

And that's where he ended his days, living to his hundredth birthday! Slim left a memorable record as an outstanding trapper and trader.

Scotty Gaul

In His Many Years He Saw It All

Scotty Gaul beat all the Hudson Bay Company traders on the Arctic Coast for longevity. He worked at various Company posts from 1938 to 1988. A Scotsman, he loved to play golf and would drive orange-painted golf balls over the Arctic snows.

* * *

When Scotty initially signed up with the Hudson Bay Company, he signed a contract for a yearly salary of twenty-four pounds sterling, a common practice at that time. When he operated their trading post at Bernard Harbour north of Coppermine in 1928, an Italian by the name of Count Bezone brought in a Ford truck with tracks instead of wheels: an innovation years ahead of its time and the first motor-driven vehicle in the Arctic. For some reason it never worked as well as expected and was left behind the police barracks at Bernard Harbour, where I saw it as late as 1990.

Scotty told me that Bezone, then about sixty years old, got sick at Bernard Harbour and died suddenly. Most likely he got the flu during the great flu epidemic that penetrated the North. After his widow had buried him there, she and her one child left the area, going west with Nels Vhatum in his schooner.

The first night out, after they had pitched their tent on the beach, it caught fire and burned when Nels accidentally set fire to ten gallons of naphtha. Poor Countess Bezone was being plagued by misfortune.

Fire seemed to be a recurring hazard on the Arctic Coast. Patsy, son of the famous trader Christian Klinkenberg, left Scotty's post at Perry River one time in his schooner *Aklavik* and went to Cambridge Bay to get a load of supplies for his trading post at Wilmot Island. It was cold, being the fall of the year, and Patsy had trouble starting his engine. He was using a blowtorch to warm it up when he caused an explosion that killed him, injured his son, Ielik, and burned up his boat. The famous bush pilot Ernie Boffa flew Ielik to Aklavik hospital in his Norseman aircraft and saved his life.

Scotty told of the Hudson Bay Company manager Paddy Gibson who was taking a planeload of fur south with pilot Alf Kaywood, who later became the chief pilot for Eldorado Mine. Kaywood was forced to land on Dismal Lake, south of Coppermine, when a cigarette ignited some fuel leaking from cans on board. They lost most of their fur.

In those early years in the North, the radio station KDKA in Pittsburgh started regular Saturday evening broadcasts to the Arctic, which the isolated northerners listened to faithfully. Later, the Canadian Broadcasting Corporation carried on this service, moving it to Friday evenings and having announcer Norm Nicholright transmit messages. It became a widespread favourite party line of information.

Scotty finally moved to Vancouver Island, where he passed on when he was in his nineties. I visited him there and we spent an afternoon reminiscing about life in the North and its unforgettable characters.

My Friend
Captain Pedersen

By Sail, Steam and Diesel, He Did It All

During my frequent visits to the Arctic Coast, the Eskimos showed me many brass telescopes, brass-bound trunks, plus many schooners. They said all had come from a Captain Pedersen, who used to whale and trade in their territory. I decided I must contact this outstanding individual. I located him in Pacifica, California.

We soon struck up a correspondence that lasted from 1962 to 1967. In his letters he told me of many Arctic voyages, most of which he seems to have spent in the crow's nest, scouting ahead for leads in the ice.

* * *

Captain Pedersen

Captain Christian Theodore Pedersen started out in 1894 as an apprentice seaman and harpooner aboard the steam barque whaler *Fearless*. In 1913, his ship *Elvira* was crushed by ice off the coast of Alaska. He escaped to dry land with his crew and then mushed south by dog team 630 miles to Fairbanks. In 1924, his trading schooner *Nanuk* was pirated by Russian Cossacks off the Siberian coast. He was held prisoner for several days before being released, but lost his $20,000 cargo of trade goods.

When the whaling industry declined early in the twentieth century, the Captain switched to trading with the Eskimos for white fox, ivory and polar bear hides. He outfitted many free traders along the Arctic Coast and sailed up from San Francisco for twenty-one consecutive years, ending in 1936.

Every year he carried several schooners on the deck of his ship the *Patterson*, offloading most of them at Herschel Island off the coast of the Yukon. On two trips he brought food and medicine to the starving and sick residents of Point Barrow, Alaska. His wife, a registered nurse, travelled with him, assisting the Natives.

In 1967 I decided to meet the famous captain in person. I found him and his wife in their seaside bungalow in Pacifica. At ninety years old, the Captain was busy cutting trees on his property with a chainsaw! Besides that, he was cleaning polar bear hides for resale to Japan for use in making fishing lures. He told me he had bought two hundred hides that year, mostly from Russia, and was getting a dollar per square inch for them.

Looking around, I saw on the wall of his living room his license to captain ships in sail, steam and diesel. He had done it all. In one memorable voyage under sail between San Francisco and Alaska he had broken a record for speed.

The Captain met his end two years later under terrifying circumstances. Two young convicts escaped from jail in nearby San Bruno and broke into the Pedersen house. The couple, who had gone to bed, were savagely beaten, evidently in an attempt to find out where they kept their money. A neighbour called the police, who arrived in force. With the help of trained dogs, they apprehended the culprits under the house. The Captain and his seventy-four-year-old wife were put in an ambulance, but he died en route to the hospital. His wife's skull was fractured, but she survived. June 20, 1969, marked the end of a legend and the loss of a friend I greatly admired.

Jake Jacobson

The Russian Trader

Jake was born in Siberia, Russia, in 1878, so he was already 78 years old when I talked to him in 1956. I carried a tape recorder up to his room in the Catholic hospital in Aklavik and got him to tell me the story of his eventful life.

* * *

When he was young, Jake Jacobson and a partner got an eight-ton schooner that operated under sail and began trading with the local Natives of the Siberian Coast. He was making wood alcohol, which he was trading for sable and white fox pelts. He also engaged in the illegal trade for walrus ivory.

He told of one trip when they were boarded by a pair of Cossacks, who were intending to arrest them. Jake was able to get them to join a shore party and, by furnishing plenty of alcohol, kept them drunk for three days until he and his partner were able to set sail at night and make their escape. However, the wind died and it was touch and go for several anxious hours.

Jake carried on this illegal trade on the Siberian Coast until 1910, when he sailed across the Bering Strait to Nome, Alaska. There he continued his trading with the Eskimos along the coast of that American state. He continued working his way east to Herschel Island off the coast of the Yukon. He built himself a log cabin out of driftwood, married an Eskimo by the name of Vera Keuna Nuviliana, and started raising a family. By this time plastics had replaced whalebone for buggy whips, fishing rods and corset stays and the whaling industry was petering out anyway. So Jake joined the many trappers who were after white fox. He worked his way farther east and put up a small shack on Booth Island, just west of Cape Parry. Here he found the white fox plentiful and soon had over five hundred, using only fifteen traps.

On the other hand, he found himself running out of grub with a wife and eight kids to feed. The carcasses of the fox – as well as his dog team – kept them from starving. But fox proved a very lean diet. His wife Vera managed to make salt by boiling seawater. Finally Jake, along with his two

neighbours, Ted Ainsly and Patsy Wyant, decided
to mush forty-five miles southwest to the mouth of
the Horton River, where Fritz Wolki had a small
trading post. When they got there, they discovered
they were not alone in their troubles.

Fritz Wolki had been a Kaiser guard in Germany
before migrating north. At age sixty-five he was still
in top shape and boasted that he even walked the
forty-five miles to Booth Island in a single day. Besides his son, Jim, and wife, Vera, Jake employed
a dwarf Eskimo named Mongolana, whom he had
sent out twelve miles by dog team to set a seal net.
But when Mongolana went back after two days to
check the net he couldn't find it. So Fritz and Jim
went back with him to search for it.

As the three of them were looking for the net,
the ice they were on broke off from the pack and
began to drift. They were forced to spend the night
out there in a hastily built igloo with no heat and
no food. In the morning they found that the a hundred and fifty yards of open water had frozen over
with about an inch-and-a-half of new ice. The two
younger men got up their courage and managed to
run across to solid ice. That left Fritz with his dog
team. He soon tried to follow them, but his dogs
broke through the thin ice, became entangled in
their harness and drowned. Fritz was left in the water
clawing like a stricken bear at the edge of the hole.

Arctic fox

It took him too long to finally roll himself up on the fragile ice. By this time he was thoroughly soaked. In fact he was so convinced that he would freeze to death that in desperation he tried to wrench a rifle from Jake's son's grasp so he could shoot himself. But Jim, resisting him, held on to it.

Taking the rifle with him, Jim ran the twelve miles back to their cabin. They estimated the temperature at -50°F. Vera immediately harnessed her three dogs and took off to rescue Fritz. It took about three hours for her to return with him; by then he was badly frozen. Gangrene set in and over the following week the pain became so unbearable that the old captain Wolki shot himself on the eleventh day.

This was the sad news that greeted Jake and his companions when they arrived at the camp. They traded some fox pelts for the few trade goods available and returned to Booth Island.

Following these incidents, Jake moved his family west to the mouth of the Anderson River, where he built a log cabin on Wood Bay. After a couple of years trapping in the area, the family moved east three hundred miles to the mouth of Inman River between Paulatuk and Coppermine. There he opened a trading post for the Hudson Bay Company. His final move was taking his family in his small schooner back to the Mackenzie Delta and settling in Aklavik. When E-3 (later called Inuvik) was built in 1955, Jake got the job of delivering government liquor to the new town site, thirty-five miles across the delta. I can remember seeing his schooner tied up to the bank of the river close to my little shack on Friday nights as he dispensed liquor to those who presented their liquor permits. It was the right job for an old-timer who had started his career trading wood alcohol to the Natives along the Siberian Coast.

Paul Steen

Robinson Crusoe of the Arctic Coast

Born on a homestead in Texas in 1894, Paul Steen started his trapping career taking coyotes, skunks and opossums on his father's farm. When he was in his late teens, the Steen family moved by covered wagon to San Diego, where Paul spotted a four-master schooner in the harbour. It was loading salt for a voyage to Seattle; he signed aboard as a "work-a-way," which paid $1 for the trip. In Seattle the ship was loaded with cargo for several Alaskan ports. Paul signed on there as an ordinary seaman for $25 a month. After unloading at Point Barrow on the northern tip of Alaska, the boat was punctured by an ice floe and had to be beached six miles south, never to sail again.

Although he was my father-in-law, I never met Paul Steen. But having been married to one of his daughters for over thirty-five years now, I have a pretty good idea of the kind of man he was. And the more I learned of him, the more my admiration grew.

* * *

Paul went to work 'floor whaling' for the famous Charlie Brower at Point Barrow, which meant that he was put on a crew using a *umiak* – a large, open wood-framed boat covered by walrus skins – used to hunt whales in the ice-strewn waters of the northern seas. During the next two years he met members of the Canadian Arctic Expedition, including their leader, Vilhjalmur Stefansson.

Then Paul met an Alaskan named Alec Allen who had a schooner loaded with freight for Herschel Island and Bernard Harbour far to the east. Paul joined Allen for the voyage and ended up spending the winter at Pierce Point trapping white fox. He was twenty-one years old. He put up a small shack at Keats Point east of Pierce Point and, without dogs, travelled his trapline on foot, dragging a small hand sled.

During that winter he suffered from the dreaded scurvy, as he had little fresh meat. He subsisted mostly on the carcasses of the white fox he trapped, soaked in brine. When the ice melted on the Arctic Ocean that next summer, Paul rowed his dory back to Pierce Point and rejoined Allen. They sailed back to Herschel Island for supplies and Paul acquired a dog team. He also met an Alaskan named Pete Lockerston, with whom he spent the following winter trapping from an Island in the Mackenzie River Delta.

During a sled trip around Christmas, Paul got caught in a vicious snowstorm and froze both feet. He was crippled for the rest of the winter. Luckily he had Pete with him to cut firewood and do the outside chores.

The following summer, while at Herschel for a resupply, Paul joined up with Scotty McIntyre, who had the fifty-foot schooner *Argo*. They sailed east and wintered at Cape Parry. An Alaskan Native named One-Arm-Johnny teamed up with Paul to trap. The price of white fox had jumped from six dollars to forty-five dollars apiece! The next summer Paul accompanied Scotty east of Coppermine to Tree River. They tried trapping the next winter, but found the area poor for white fox. Paul returned to Cape Parry by dog team just before the ice went out. The next winter Paul got two hundred and twenty-five foxes, which he sold for thirty dollars apiece. With the proceeds he bought himself a whale boat, and used it to take his dogs and outfit to Roscoe River, about fifty miles east of Pierce Point, where he spent the winter in his boat. After trapping ninety-eight foxes and shooting one polar bear, he waited for open water and then sailed back to Pierce Point to wait for a trader.

At Pierce Point that summer Paul met the Russian trapper Jake Jacobson. One of Jake's daughters was sixteen-year-old Elizabeth, called Bessie by her family; her Eskimo name was Siliona. There developed a strong attachment between Paul and Bessie that summer. Before freeze-up Jake moved his family back to his camp at Inman River toward Coppermine, and Paul accompanied them in his own schooner.

Jake moved back into his cabin on the east side of the Inman River while Paul put up a tent across on the west side. At the same time a Danish trapper by the name of Henry Jensen moved in and set up his tent next to Paul's. He, too, was interested in Bessie.

Captain Henry Larsen of the RCMP schooner *St. Roche* had hired Jake several times as an ice captain for his boat and would often stop at Inman River. Later he wrote a book entitled *The Big Ship*. In its twenty-sixth chapter, entitled *Eskimo Love and Drama*, he describes an interesting incident involving Bessie and her two suitors. According to Larsen, the two young trappers were in the habit of crossing the river to court Bessie. Jake's wife, Vera, had been raised on Herschel Island, where the American whaling ships often wintered. There she developed a deep-seated suspicion of the intentions of white suitors. This prejudice became evident on one occasion when she objected to the conduct of the Dane. She drove Jensen out of her camp with a loaded shotgun in such a hurry that he was obliged to swim the river back to his camp. She even discharged the gun at him several times, forcing him to dive like a seal!

The predictable outcome of the summer's amorous activities was Paul's victory. He succeeded in convincing Vera of his honourable intentions and, although twice Bessie's age, was accepted as her suitor. In August 1931, he took her to Coppermine, where they were married.

They moved back to Inman River and set up housekeeping in a small shack next to the Jacobsons. In spite of her youth, Bessie turned out to be the ideal trapper's wife. But firewood was scarce and Paul was forced to go forty-five miles to get it. He had to go six miles out on the ocean ice to hunt seals for dog feed. He trapped only 60 fox that winter, but stayed another winter to keep his young wife near her parents. She got pregnant almost immediately and, worried about giving birth, persuaded Paul to take her to the hospital in Aklavik 300 miles west. They left on the first of March 1932, each driving a separate team, and arrived on the fifth of April after a gruelling trip. The baby was born the following day.

Paul left Bessie and the baby in Aklavik and drove his team back to Inman River alone, arriving in the middle of June, just before the ice began to candle and break up. He took down their lumber house, loaded the boards on his schooner and sailed west to Baillie Island, where he was reunited with his wife.

They went in their schooner to the mouth of the Anderson River where Paul rebuilt their house. He spent the following winter trapping in this new area. There were plenty of moose, but he took only sixty foxes, many of them coloured. Then his father-in-law, Jake, showed up and persuaded Paul to go upriver trapping while he and his family moved into Paul's cabin at the mouth. It proved costly for Paul and his family. They went upriver thirty miles to a place called Husky Bend, but there was no place to haul out the schooner where it would be safe from the ice coming downstream in the spring breakup. Paul built a log cabin, but had no luck either hunting or trapping. He and his growing family kept alive by eating cranberries and the carcasses of the muskrats they caught. His dog team, weak from starvation, couldn't work. The river rose twenty feet in the spring and the ice came down and took their schooner with it. As soon as they could get out in open water they rowed their small skiff back down to the ocean. Only one sled dog survived.

Paul had to start all over again. With Jake and his family living in his first cabin, Paul had to cut logs and build a new one. It was there that my wife, Margaret, was born on February 12, 1945.

Luckily the Roman Catholic Church had put up a new mission nine miles away at a place called Stanton. The mission also kept a small store, so the following winter was not so bad. Paul, with his family in a new log cabin, resumed trapping and got several moose. The following year Bessie was expecting another baby. When her time drew near, they decided to take the whole family by dog team to Aklavik, a trip of two hundred miles.

Returning with the new baby from Aklavik, the family spent the next winter at Pierce Point, a hundred miles north of the settlement of Paulatuk. On his many trips there Paul had noticed the country around Brock River, halfway between these two places, and decided to give it a try. Taking his family, which now included half a dozen children, and a new dog team he had acquired, he rowed down there and put up a tent. They were on a sand spit between the Brock River lagoon and the ocean, a very exposed location. Paul expected to take his family back to Pierce Point in the fall, but he never did. He found a coal seam two miles inland – which was as good as a gold mine – so they had a handy source of fuel. He blasted the coal out with black powder and hauled it with his dogs. The kids kept busy patrolling the beach looking for driftwood. There were Arctic char in the river running right by their tent, and occasionally caribou or musk ox would wander within rifle shot. The kids also picked low bush cranberries and set traps for ground squirrels.

In the winter it was a different story. The snow drifted right up to the peak of their tent. They had one kerosene lamp, which Bessie would hang outside on a pole if she was expecting Paul back from his trapline. She feared he might go right by the tent without seeing it.

The babies kept coming, but Paul now had too many children to take them all to Aklavik for the arrival of yet another, so he delivered them himself. As the years rolled along and his family increased, Paul kept adding to their tent. He found an abandoned trapper's shack along the coast, which he dismantled and used for an addition. He put a window in the roof so they could get some light in when the snow drifted up over the walls, but during the long, dark winter there wasn't much light in the sky and they had to depend on their one kerosene lantern. They ended up with fourteen children. Try to imagine all those kids confined indoors day after day with no toys or schoolbooks to keep them occupied. This accomplishment merits special praise.

Their isolation was compounded by the fact that Paul was determined to live off the land in an age that had not yet seen any social services. This feat could not now be repeated even in the most remote areas of the Arctic. The family suffered, too,

Paul Steen's daughter Margaret harvesting cranberries. The dogs are there to scare off bears.

by the fact that they had no neighbours to help. After spending their childhood under these conditions, any future life had to be an improvement. The Steen children passed the test.

At Christmas, however, Paul managed to take the whole family by dogsled to their nearest neighbours at Paulatuk. They slept on the floor of the mission courtesy of Father Léonce DeHurtevent, an Oblate priest. It was there that these children saw their first oranges and were given their first toys. All too soon they were on their way back to their tent at Brock River, not to return until the next Christmas rolled around.

With all these mouths to feed Paul was under constant pressure to get game. There were times when he was delayed and Bessie was forced to boil up any old scraps of hides to keep her brood alive. But when the older boys got big enough to travel with dogs, Paul had some help. Then, in the early 1950s, Bessie started acting strangely, talking to people who were not there. Paul became alarmed and sent her to the doctors in Aklavik. They sent her to a mental institution in Calgary where she remained, never returning to her family, never seeing Paul again.

With Bessie gone, Paul found himself unable to look after his children and continue trapping, his only source of income, so he sent them to the

Catholic hostel in Aklavik. Once they were gone, Paul quit Brock River and moved back to Pierce Point with two of the older boys who were working for the new Distant Early Warning Line. He built himself a small lumber shack and resumed trapping white fox.

One day, when it was -50°F, Paul returned to his shack with his dog team after visiting his traps. He rushed into the shack and started a wood fire in the stove. He had no sooner gotten back to unload his sled and unhitch his dogs when the shack erupted in flames. He stood helplessly by as it burned to the ground. All he salvaged was on the sled. It was the last straw!

At that juncture in his life, without a wife, without a tent, with his children grown or gone, he quit trapping and drove his dogs west to the Eskimo village of Tuktoyaktuk. There he acquired another small schooner in which he lived. He was two miles from the town, alone after all those years being surrounded by his large family. But he didn't complain and he didn't expect any government assistance. Sometimes he would walk up to the mission, where he would say a prayer in the chapel. One winter's day in 1969, two friends walked out from town to visit him. They found him dead, frozen on the ground among his sled dogs. He had been cutting up driftwood with a swede saw to heat his boat and

apparently died of a heart attack. He was seventy-
five years old.

Paul Steen could be compared to Robinson
Crusoe, that fictional character of Daniel Defoe's
imagination, whose epic journeys captured the
imagination of generations of readers. Nowadays,
with all the government social workers in the North,
nobody goes hungry. That Brock River Robinson
Crusoe–type of life is now history.

Father Léonce DeHurtevent o.m.i.

The Saint of Paulatuk

During the last century-and-a-half, there have been hundreds of Oblate missionaries working in the Canadian Arctic, but none have merited the title of "saint" as much as Father Léonce Dehurtevent OMI. He earned it the hard way.

* * *

Léonce Dehurtevent was born in France in 1911, ordained a priest in 1936, and sent to the Canadian north the following year. For the next fifty-eight years he lived among the Eskimos, spending forty-eight of them at Paulatuk, a small settlement on the Arctic Ocean between Tuktoyaktuk and Coppermine. His first task was to

learn the Eskimo language, as well as English. Only
then did he begin to learn the art of living in this
land of ice and snow, including the mastery of driving a dog team.

The church decided to build a permanent mission at Paulatuk in the early 1930s because a seam of
coal had been found ten miles east at the mouth of
the Hornaday River. In fact, the very name for the
place in Eskimo, "Paula," means soot or coal. Léonce
not only helped build it but lived in it for nearly
half a century, except for a couple of years in the
mid-fifties, when a Distant Early Warning site was
being built at Cape Parry ninety miles north. Drawn
there by the work available, all the people left
Paulatuk, and their pastor followed them, accompanied by a young Oblate named André Vermaut.
These two put up a small plywood cabin among the
shacks that were hurriedly built by the natives with
scraps they had found in the dump. After the DEW
Line site was built, the Eskimos drove their dog
teams back to Paulatuk, and Léonce moved back
into his mission.

But Bishop Joseph Trocellier had sent me down
to Cape Parry the winter before to discuss with
Léonce the feasibility of tearing down the Paulatuk
Mission and moving it to Cape Parry using the
Mission's supply schooner, *Notre Dame de Lourdes*. I
spent three nights with Léonce and André sharing

the monotonous diet of potatoes and wieners they had scavenged from the DEW Line dump. Besides talking, we spent those three days putting down fibreglass over their ceiling to help conserve their heat. Back at Paulatuk, Léonce and his companion resumed their work of netting fish under the ice to feed their dogs, and blasting out coal at their mine to heat the mission.

After nine years, André had had enough and returned to France, leaving Léonce alone again. He not only helped the Eskimos build small plywood shacks, but was always available to fill in on their local jobs when they went out on the land to hunt.

By this time I had moved from Inuvik and built a mission at Colville Lake, a hundred and fifty miles south of Paulatuk. I had also been given a Cessna 180 aircraft that enabled me to fly down to Paulatuk for frequent visits.

On one of our first flying visits, which was to last a week, my wife, Margaret, had prepared a ham, a turkey and assorted baked goods, including bread, pies and cakes. On our first evening there, we accompanied Léonce to his quonset hut church next door to attend the five o'clock Mass. Of course the mission was always open and the people took advantage of a makeshift honey bucket in a back room of the mission adjacent to the kitchen. They discovered all the goodies we had just brought and

Father Léonce DeHurtevent, OMI

made short work of them. We spent the week sharing Léonce's standard diet of bannock, char and caribou.

Noting that his kitchen utensils were ancient and badly worn, we sent Léonce a new set of silverware for Christmas. The following summer I flew the new bishop, Paul Piché, to Paulatuk for his annual pastoral visit. At the table I noticed that we were using the same old utensils we thought we had replaced. I asked Léonce where the new silverware was, and he admitted that he had hidden it because he felt that his flock would quickly borrow it for their own tables.

When television made its debut, the church sent a new unit to Léonce, but he soon lent it out and returned to his radio. All the missions were equipped with a Marconi transceiver with which they kept in touch with the mother mission at Fort Smith. We had a nightly sched at seven p.m. One time Léonce went off the air for a week. When he returned he told me that the kids, playing in his room, had accidentally tuned off his frequency, and it took him a week to notice.

The church also sent Léonce a sixteen-foot aluminum boat with which he could visit his nets. On one visit I noticed that it was gone. Léonce pointed out to me a tiny speck on an island a mile away and said, "That's my boat. I guess the kids forgot to tie it up after playing with it. But that's okay, I know just where to get it."

The church sent him a skidoo another year. I noticed it parked in his porch and asked why he wasn't using it. He explained that he had loaned the motor to one of the Eskimos whose motor had quit.

In later years he was equipped with a four-wheel ATV with which he would meet me at the airstrip when I flew in. On one trip I noticed that he was walking, so I asked about his vehicle. He explained that he had loaned it to a local hunter who had abandoned it out on the tundra when it ran out of gas. "No problem," said Léonce. "It's only twenty miles out and we're going to carry some gas out there next week."

Léonce's philosophy of life did not admit of problems. His flock of Eskimos were essentially blameless, no matter what their shortcomings.

When Paulatuk's population soared over one hundred, they formed a co-op. But the Eskimo in charge had difficulties denying credit to his relatives and friends, which included just about everyone. Soon the accounts receivable soared to a quarter of a million dollars, and the suppliers stopped shipping groceries and hardware. The Co-op was dead. Léonce explained to me that this happened because of the charitable character of the Eskimos, who simply could not say no to someone in want.

In only one instance did I note that Léonce was disappointed with his people, and that followed his unsuccessful attempt to get them to sign a petition to stop the heavy traffic in liquor coming in on their weekly scheduled aircraft from Inuvik, two hundred and sixty miles to the west. It didn't break his heart, but it did limit his ability to protect his people from something he knew was undermining their inherently good moral lives.

Another thing that annoyed Léonce was the prevalence of Sunday picnics away from the community that kept some of his parishioners from attending church services. But at the same time he sympathized with them.

Léonce was never openly critical of anyone, especially his flock. He found an excuse for any misdemeanor. He realized that the people had only recently emerged from the stone age and that Christianity introduced a whole new set of guidelines they would need time to assimilate. Although they had always believed in a god, Léonce told me that they had never imagined a son of God – Christ and his redemption.

Léonce Dehurtevent was not only a faithful pastor of his flock, but a shining example to his fellow missionaries. When he died on April 6, 2002, one of his parishioners wrote, "I want to thank the Church for having let Father live and pray with us for so many years."

Jeanne and Johnnie Branson

Adventurers and Entrepreneurs

Jeanne was born in Belgium in 1918 while her parents were prisoners of the Germans. She was the third of eight children. The family later escaped to Canada and settled in Edmonton. When she was eleven, a friend of her father's gave her a lion cub. This triggered a love for wild animals that resulted in her acquiring tigers, bears, gorillas, and other creatures. While still a teenager, Jeanne joined Loews Circus and toured the world. In 1942 she met and soon married Johnnie, a motorcycle speed demon. He held the world record and pioneered the risky trick of roaring around the inside of a steel mesh globe. He even persuaded Jeanne to ride on his shoulders.

Johnnie later bought a cargo freighter boat and sailed to the East Indies, Sumatra and the Philippines, picking up all sorts of wild animals, which he sold to zoos and circuses. Working out of Los Angeles, he was soon exhibiting animals across the States. He told me of one incident on the east coast when a four thousand–lb sea elephant got sick and he had to rent a U-Haul trailer to lug it back to Los Angeles. Crossing Ohio, it died, so he pulled off the highway and drove into a farmer's orchard. There he tied the critter to a fruit tree and drove off. He said he wished he could have seen the farmer when he discovered that enormous creature tied to one of his trees.

Around 1942, the Bransons bought up the land on the east shore of Great Bear Lake that had once been the site of the settlement of Port Radium and built Branson's Fishing Lodge. It became a great success, mainly due to Jeanne's promotion work in the off-season. She toured all the sportsmen's shows across the United States in her white Tornado sports car, and appeared on many TV shows displaying a huge mounted lake trout and a world-record twenty-lb Arctic char that she had caught herself.

Jeanne loved hunting and managed to bag a polar bear in the far North and a Kodiak bear in

Alaska. She had the Kodiak mounted but he was so tall she had to have a hole cut in her ceiling to accommodate his head. She also trained sled dogs for harness.

In 1966 she visited me at Colville Lake after I had built the log church dedicated to Our Lady of the Snows. Noticing that I didn't have a bell for it, she kept an eye out for one. The next winter, on her promotion tour for the lodge, she found a bell in Indianola, Iowa, outside Desmoines, and delivered it to my dock in her Norseman aircraft the following summer. At a thousand lbs it was the biggest bell in the Northwest Territories.

In order to keep Johnnie busy during the winter, they had bought fifteen acres of land along the Colorado River near Parker, Arizona, in 1946. This property they developed into another lodge and trailer park. They sold their Great Bear lodge around 1972; subsequent owners were not able to equal Jeannie's success, so it was abandoned and finally burned by unknown arsonists in 1999.

At age eighty-eight Jeanne is still actively running her lodge on the Colorado River with a staff of eight. She has had attractive offers to buy it, but says, "And then what would I do?" What an amazing woman!

Simon Bashaw

White Russian Trapper

Of all the trappers working in the North in the twentieth century, one of the most fascinating was Simon Bashaw, who claimed to be a White Russian. Simon, whom I describe in detail in my book *Arctic Journal*, had married a woman who was an excellent trapper in her own right. Simon was the last northerner I ever saw wearing the old-style beaded leggings.

* * *

Simon Bashaw emigrated from Russia and ended up at Fort Chipewyan, on the western end of Lake Athabaska in northern Alberta. There he met and married his Chipewyan wife and moved east to begin trapping on Colin River.

The first log cabin he built was just long enough to accommodate a short bunk and had a single

10″ x 12″ pane of glass for a window. But he built a commodious gazebo for his dog team that was unique in the North. Its spacious, spruce bough–covered roof kept the snow off all his dogs chained beneath.

The following year he built a proper-sized log cabin that had an interesting interior. The first thing one would notice was that the floor was covered with empty tin cans. Simon explained that once he had had a visit from a neighbouring trapper who asked for an empty can he could use during the night to answer a call of nature. Simon looked in vain for one, and then and there vowed to himself that he would never be caught short again. He had been saving empty cans for years.

Then there was the radio at the head of Simon's bunk. Simon read at night in bed by the light of candles placed on top of the radio. It was now completely covered in wax except for two holes to the tuning knobs. Simon read nothing but geology and said he knew every rock for miles around. He was available to guide propectors and charged $200 per day. "That might seem high," he said, "but not when you realize that I can lead you to a producing minesite." To date no one had taken advantage of his knowledge.

Simon Bashaw

I was intrigued by the dog bells hanging on the outside of all the windows. Simon explained that they were hung there to scare away the bears.

Simon appreciated the fact that I was a man of the cloth. He confessed that he seldom prayed but added that when he did pray he got an immediate answer. He cited two such incidents when he was out travelling with his dog team.

During World War II he had heard that his countryman Stalin was engaged in the war, and decided to offer to help. So he directed a prayer to heaven when he was camped out one night. Immediately, a beautiful male figure clothed in white walked up to his fire and asked, "Simon, did you call me?"

Without waking, Simon knew he was face to face with Christ. "Yes," replied Simon, "I've been reading about the terrible war in my homeland and I wanted to volunteer my services to go back and speak to Stalin about ending this conflict and bloodshed." According to Simon, Christ thanked him for his offer and promised that he would call on Simon if it became necessary. He never did.

Another time, while Simon was camped out for the night with his sled dogs chained around him, he was bothered by a pack of wolves circling his camp. The constant whimpering of his dogs was keeping him awake, so as a last resort he offered up a prayer. Just then a figure in green walked up to his fire to ask if he had called. Simon asked, "Are you Christ?" but the heavenly figure answered, "No, Simon, I'm the Archangel Michael. What can I do for you?"

Simon explained how the pack of wolves was harassing him. Without another word, the angel beckoned to his companions, who were standing just out of the firelight. They each took hold of a wolf by the scruff of the neck and led them away. "That's the last time wolves ever bothered me," concluded Simon.

It was late at night by candlelight in Simon's cabin when he was recounting these strange incidents to me and the atmosphere was not a little creepy. Then Simon, bringing his face up close to mine, whispered, "Are you thinking I'm a little bushed?"

"Of course not, Simon," I replied as convincingly as I could under the circumstances, though I doubt there was much conviction in my voice. As we drove our dogs out of his camp the next day, we were certain we had visited one of the North's unusual characters.

In the fall of the year, Phillip and I, along with two Cree boys, had spent a couple of weeks fishing with gill nets off Spider Island, about three miles from Simon's cabin. We caught hundreds of trout and white fish for our winter's supply of dog feed, which we left hanging on wooden racks high above the ground. During the winter I returned there alone with my team to get a load. As it was too late in the evening to return to Camsell Portage, I decided to spend the night with Simon. When I got to his cabin I found it empty but unlocked. I tied up my dogs under his handy gazebo, carried my gear into the cabin and built a fire. After a good supper of caribou meat I was relaxing with my pipe when I thought I heard a dog bark. Thinking Simon was returning, I went outside to listen. There it was again, down toward the lake.

I started to follow a well-beaten trail and could soon see a dim light in a cabin window. I didn't know that Simon's wife lived in a separate cabin a hundred and fifty yards away. But I soon found her after breaking the file she had used to bar her door. She couldn't open it herself as she was bedridden. I soon found out that she had fallen through the thin ice covering the river nearby and caught a cold that developed into pneumonia. After a week with no improvement she told her husband that the only thing to cure her would be a fresh young caribou. So he took off with his dog team to find one, leaving his wife as comfortable as possible. Her three huskies were chained outside the door. She was in her feather robe on the floor next to the wood stove, with a stack of kindling by her side and sacks of flour, sugar and rolled oats under her head and some blocks of ice nearby. Unfortunately, she had experienced a bout of delirium that rendered her unconscious. She had rolled against the red-hot stove and burned one leg, rendering her immobile. She had been unable to move outside to feed her dogs, and Simon had been gone a week. The bark I had heard had to be very feeble.

When I got back to Camsell Portage the next day with my sledload of fish I sent a message to the Royal Canadian Mounted Police at Uranium City. The RCMP promptly flew to Simon's camp at Colin River and took his wife to the hospital. It took them another week to locate Simon at his tent camp to the North, still waiting for caribou.

Later I heard more from the Natives about this tiny Chipewyan woman. I was dealing with one tough cookie. She had been married to Simon for forty years, but they had only lived together two weeks when he objected to her cooking. He fixed up a warehouse for her and she moved in there. The separation only strengthened their marriage, according to Simon. "We've never had any arguments," he told me later. "Some evenings I go over there to visit and some evenings she comes over here," he said. They were together yet separate even when travelling. If they went by boat, he towed her behind his motorboat in her hunting canoe. If they were travelling in winter, she followed his team with her own dogs and toboggan. Each traded his or her own furs and bought his or her own separate grub supplies. They never had any children.

His wife also held her own in the bush, hunting and trapping. She wore a white canvas parka that was all but invisible against the snowy background. The Cree Indians feared her, so she had no friend by her husband. They were seen together infrequently when they came to the Hudson Bay Store at Camsell Portage to sell their furs.

When Simon's wife eventually died, the police went to clear out her cabin. They were amazed to find stashed under the floorboards many items new from the store that she had hoarded, such as axes, rifles, bolts of cloth, and so on. Simon wanted none of it and had it donated to the Mission at Fort Chipewyan.

One time Simon brought me his .30-.30 rifle that had a shell stuck in the barrel. I got it out without much trouble. When he came back to get it he remarked, "If you hadn't gone into the ministry, you could have been a real success!" That was my lesson in humility for the day.